WHERE DO PROFITS COME FROM?

THE ROAD TO ECONOMIC PROSPERITY

RICK D. PUGLISI

Although the author and publisher have made every effort to ensure that the information in this book was correct at press time, the author and publisher do not assume and hereby disclaim any liability to any party for any loss, damage, or disruption caused by errors or omissions, whether such errors or omissions result from negligence, accident, or any other cause.

Cover Illustration by PSDGraphics

DEDICATION

This book is dedicated to Francesco and Joseph. The financial world is difficult to understand, but with a little guidance and understanding, I hope you will navigate safely through any turmoil.

TABLE OF CONTENTS

LIST OF FIGURES

ACKNOWLEDGEMENTS

I would like to express my gratitude to the following people who helped me in writing this book.

Rich Coffin, who patiently read muddled manuscripts and provided detailed, insightful feedback that I consider to be invaluable. His time and effort had a huge impact on this book and his effort is greatly appreciated. Thank you so much.

Daniel Puglisi and Fred Puglisi, two wonderful brothers whose comments and insights I always value.

Most importantly, I would like to thank my wife, Yuko, and our children, Francesco and Joseph, for encouraging me and giving me the time to pursue this effort.

Chapter 1 – The Road to Economic Turmoil or Prosperity?

For the last thirty years the U.S. has been travelling on the road to economic turmoil. Its recent encounters include a tech-bubble followed by a recession in 2002, a historic housing bubble in 2007, a financial crisis in 2008, a weak and divisive recovery, and now a profit bubble that must be deflated in 2014.

The U.S. is on this road to economic turmoil because of a misunderstanding of its policies and an aversion to disruptive change that is producing a cascading series of errors. Without a proper framework, it can be difficult to determine where a country is on an economic map, how they got there, and where they are going. If a person was giving directions to a traveler who wanted to visit the coming economic turmoil it would sound something like this.

- Start with large trade deficits financed by foreign governments manipulating their currencies that take 50% to 100% of profits away from the U.S. economy.
- Next, compensate for the loss of profits by replacing these profits with a combination of excessive household debt growth and government budget deficits.
- Then, hope the banking system and mutual funds buy the excessive debt.
- Bail out investors of any government-guaranteed housing or student loan debt if these bubbles collapse along the way.
- Use central bank quantitative easing to purchase any excessive debt, finance replacement profits, and avoid a depression if interest rates are too low to induce the banks to buy the debt.

- Generate profit bubbles to counter fears that workers' skills may become stale if they are unemployed for too long after any bubble implodes.
- Increase political divisions within the country by increasing income inequality, blaming others, and advocating wealth taxes, class warfare, and other divisive solutions.
- Continue losing profits to trade deficits and compensating with unsustainable government budget deficits until total government debt approaches its final destination and either (1) inflationary demands are unleashed or (2) currency speculation and capital flight out of U.S. dollar is induced.
- Combat the inflation and/or capital flight with large increases in interest rates thus paying reparations to the currency manipulators, restoring investor confidence by forcing large doses of austerity on U.S. citizens, and entering an economic depression with an angry, divided population that is looking for someone to blame and seeking reparations as well.

It is imperative that the U.S. understands that it is on this road to economic turmoil and its future consequences. The U.S. can continue down this road for awhile without inflation or capital flight but eventually there will be a great price to pay. This road uses hope as a strategy. It ignores the large incentives for countries to not cooperate on trade and then hopes for irrational outcomes that violate game theory.

The road to economic prosperity is a much safer road. The road to economic prosperity understands where profits come from. It doesn't require housing bubbles or large government budget deficits to replace profits or quantitative easing to finance them. The road to economic prosperity starts with enforcing balanced trade by putting in place incentives for foreign governments to cooperate without punishing trade. These incentives are consistent with game theory and would foster global cooperation.

The following chapters will document the road to economic turmoil that the U.S. is currently travelling upon, illuminate several misunderstandings about profits, debt, and economic growth, and offer a solution that can change the economic course of the U.S. and foster sustainable prosperity to not only the U.S. but the entire global economy.

Trade Deficits Take Profits

Trade deficits should not be expressed as a percent of GDP but rather as a percent of profits. Every dollar in the U.S. trade deficit takes away one dollar of U.S. profits. Chapter 2 will examine this in more detail when the profit equation is discussed.

One of the misunderstandings about trade imbalances is that they are relatively unimportant. With trade deficits express as 3% of GDP it would seem that one should be more concerned about the other 97% of GDP. Yet, when that same trade deficit is expressed as 60% of sustainable profits, it acquires a sudden importance when one realizes that seeking profits is the foundation of practically 100% of our economy.

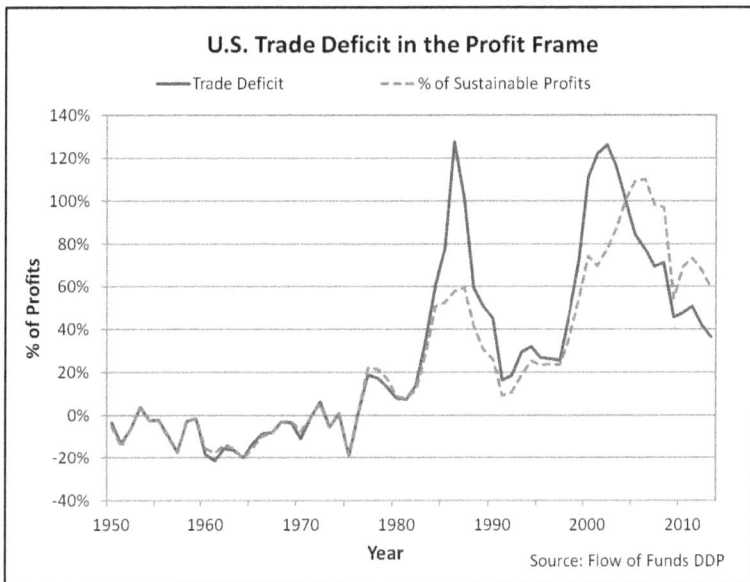

Figure 1: U.S. Trade Deficit as a Percent of Profits

Figure 1 illustrates the U.S. trade deficit since 1950 as it should be presented; as a percent of profits. Starting in the mid 1970s, the U.S. begins its journey down the road to economic turmoil with rising trade deficits. Since profits tend to fluctuate over time, the trade deficit is also expressed as a percent of sustainable after-tax profits (a constant equal to 5% of GDP). Figure 1 illustrates how detrimental trade was in the mid 1980s and how the Plaza Accords was an attempt to restore trade balance. However, once China enters the WTO in the 1990s, the U.S. trade deficit surges again and eventually consumes all of the sustainable U.S. profits peaking at 110% in 2006. While some progress has been made since 2006, the U.S. trade deficit still takes away 60% of sustainable U.S. profits as of 2013.

Figure 2 breaks the U.S. trade deficit into petroleum and non-petroleum components starting from 1994. It documents the dramatic rise in U.S. trade imbalances starting in 1998 once the world adopts an export model with currency reserves to supplement their economies. Figure 2 illustrates that the improvement in the U.S. trade deficit since 2006 is primarily due to the growth in energy production from hydraulic fracturing or "fracking". While the petroleum component has shown steady progress towards a trade balance, the non-petroleum component is reverting back to large trade imbalances exceeding 3% of GDP or 60% of sustainable profits.

The reason why the U.S. has continually run trade deficits for over thirty years is because it fails to realize that under the current economic rules of the game a country that devalues and manipulates their currency is actually paid to do so by the country running a trade deficit. Thus, rather than promoting global cooperation, the current economic rules promote economic sabotage.

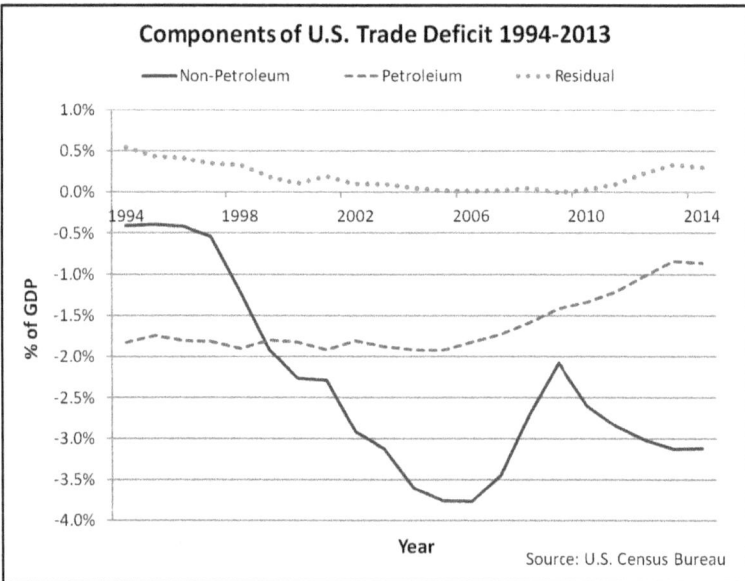

Figure 2: Components of U.S. Trade Deficit

The claim that the benefit of running a trade deficit is cheap oil or cheap goods from China is mistaken. If governments did not compensate for these trade deficits by promoting additional household debt growth and government deficits, the benefits of these cheap products would be outweighed by the cost of lost profits and the **true** cost would be exposed. Because governments compensate for the lost profits, the cost is hidden or deferred until economic crises develop and blame can be assigned to some other group that is politically convenient.

Is Currency Manipulation to Blame?

When a country runs a trade deficit, someone must lend them money to do so. Over the last thirty years it has been primarily foreign governments and their central banks that have lent money to the U.S. to finance its trade deficits. These loans are part of a government's foreign assets and are referred to as official foreign exchange reserves.

Without going too deep into the weeds, there are two offsetting parts to the Balance of Payments for a country, a current account and a capital account. The current account is the net amount of money that is entering or leaving a country due to trade or other income streams. The capital account reflects the net amount of money that is entering or leaving a country in order to invest in stocks, bonds, or tangible assets. If a country runs a current account deficit it must run a capital account surplus since they must sum to zero. The trade deficit of a country is part of the current account. The corresponding lending by foreign governments and their central banks is part of the capital account.

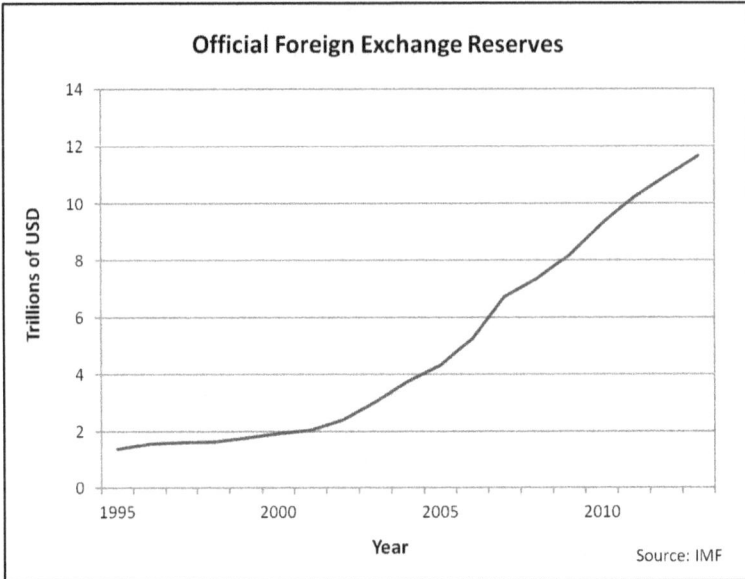

Figure 3: Official Foreign Exchange Reserves

Figure 3 shows the continuous rise in global foreign exchange reserves expressed in US dollars as the cumulative effect of the trade imbalances grows. A geographical breakdown of the foreign exchange reserves reveals that Asia owns about 60%, Europe 20%, and the Middle East 10%. The remaining 10% is distributed amongst North America, South America, and Africa.

Part of this increase is because trade has grown as a percent of global GDP and the global economy has become more open. A prudent rule for the amount of foreign exchange reserves a country should hold is to use three months of imports or exports as a benchmark (Rodrik, 2006). With a three month buffer zone or cushion, a country should be able to manage foreign exchange shocks and possible trade disruptions.

However, the growth in reserves have grown much faster than if countries were following this rule. Figure 4 shows the growth in global foreign exchange reserves in terms of months of global exports. While in 1995 the rule of three months was followed, in 2013 global foreign exchange reserves now represent over seven months of global exports.

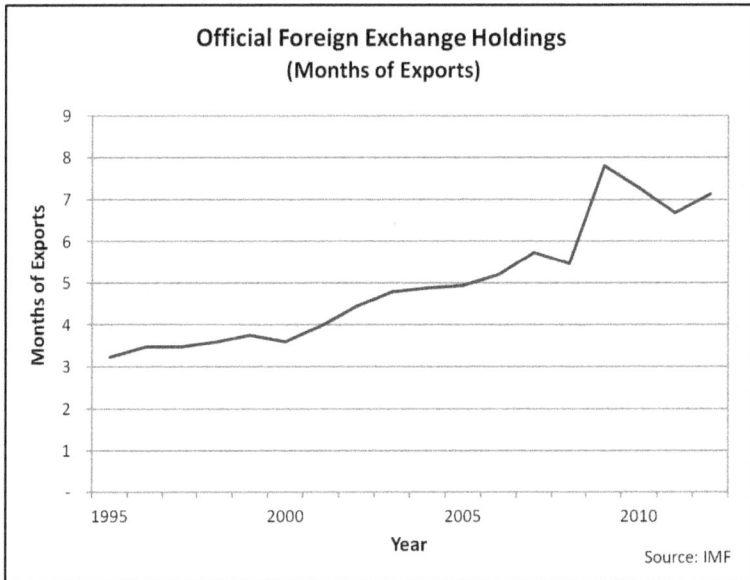

Figure 4: FX Reserves in Months of Exports

Another explanation for the growth in reserves could be because of the growing desire to invest in emerging markets or countries growing faster than the developed world. If U.S. investors overwhelm a small emerging market country with inflows of money (a.k.a. "hot money"), the emerging market country will typically counter these moves by selling domestic bonds which satisfies the demand of U.S. investors and then buying U.S. Treasuries with the proceeds which increases its foreign exchange reserves. However, picking an exchange rate that balances trade tends not to lead to long-term excessive flows spanning decades. When countries repeatedly "guess wrong", year after year, about the value of their currency that would balance trade and minimize "hot money" capital flows it is because they are manipulating their currency.

The actual reason for the growth in foreign exchange reserves is because countries that manipulate their currencies and acquire foreign reserves are actually paid to do so as we will examine in Chapter 6. Another benefit is that countries manipulating their currency are better able to maintain political control over their population by providing job security as well as additional profits to their economy.

If governments and their central banks did not finance trade deficits, the global private sector would be called upon to do so. Since banks are the main lenders in the private sector, the burden of financing the trade imbalances would fall primarily on the banks. However, to finance a trade imbalance, the banks would have to take large foreign exchange and credit risk. They would have to buy foreign assets in the currency of the deficit country with the proceeds from bank deposits redeemable in their own currency.

Imagine if every year traders in Chinese banks told their managers and investors that they were going to put on a massive $300 billion speculative foreign exchange position and each year requested to increase the size of the position to where it would now represent close to $4 trillion. This would be outrageous. Before the position surpassed $10 billion, risk managers would declare these speculative positions excessive and impose both foreign exchange and credit limits on these traders.

The risk managers understand that their banks do not have adequate capital to take large concentrated risks. With only a small change in the foreign exchange rate or default of a country, the bank would become insolvent, unable to pay their depositors in full, and have to declare bankruptcy. Without an ability to take these risks, the private sector is limited in the size of trade imbalances it can finance. Therefore, governments and their central banks are the only entities capable of financing large, recurring trade imbalances and acquiring excessive official foreign reserves.

The big question then is what comes first, the U.S. trade deficit or official foreign reserves. Is the trade deficit due to a policy of 300 million U.S. consumers deciding to buy imported products or a policy of a handful of government officials and their central bankers manipulating their currency?

The U.S. Compensates with Housing and Government Debt

If the U.S. consumer and U.S. government policy are to blame for the U.S. trade deficit and the rise in foreign exchange reserves then it would make sense that for each additional dollar of debt created by the consumer or government, something like 20% of the corresponding spending would go towards imports. This is because imports represent about 20% of national income. It would be hard to believe that if you gave a U.S. consumer one additional dollar, they would spend the entire amount on imports only.

On the other hand, if currency manipulation is to blame for the U.S. trade deficit one would expect each additional dollar of trade deficit to result in one additional dollar of U.S. debt in order to replace the profits lost from the trade deficit. Therefore, it would make sense that the additional growth of household and government debt would be one-for-one with the trade deficit.

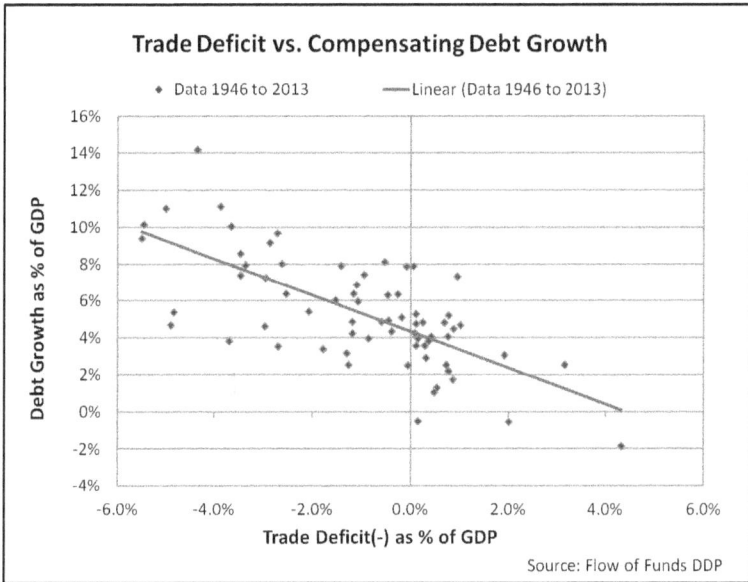

Figure 5: Trade Deficit vs. Compensating Debt Growth

Figure 5 shows the increase in annual net total debt growth of the U.S. household and government sector as a function of the U.S. trade deficit. When the U.S. has run large trade deficits, it has incurred large debt increases. When the U.S. has run trade surpluses it has incurred small debt increases. If the U.S. is to blame for its trade deficit, the slope of the regression line should be -0.2. If currency manipulation is to blame for the U.S. trade deficit, the slope should be -1.0.

A regression or linear fit of the data shows that a slope of -0.98 is the best fit with a standard error of 0.13. If the errors in the estimate of the slope are normally distributed, the difference between -0.98 and -0.2 represents 6.2 standard deviations and the probability that -0.2 is the true slope is less than one in a billion.

The data confirms that the U.S. compensates for the profits lost due to trade deficits with additional household and government debt. It thereby proves that the U.S. trade deficit is not due to the spending habits of 300 million U.S. consumers but rather due to the policies of a handful of foreign governments and their central bankers. They manipulate their currency, build foreign exchange reserves, and let the countries running

trade deficits compensate with additional debt growth or risk a
depression.

Quantitative Easing Comes to the Rescue

For every borrower there must be a lender. If the U.S. government
compensates for lost profits with additional debt growth then some
foreign or domestic lender must buy this additional debt. In the case of
currency manipulation it is usually the foreign governments who are
manipulating their currencies that are the willing buyers of this additional
debt.

However, sometimes the household sector enters a period of
deleveraging due to a financial crisis and wants to reduce consumption.
Then, the government sector must run budget deficits larger than the
trade deficit to stabilize the economy. In this case, the government must
find domestic lenders.

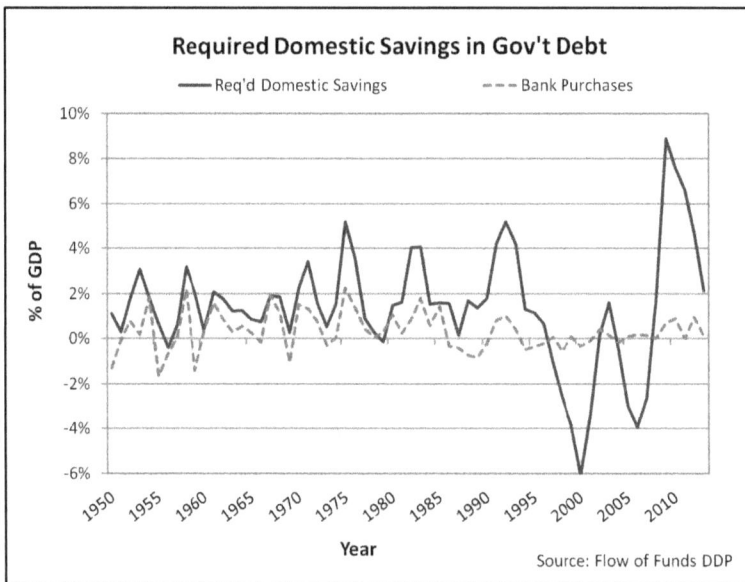

Figure 6: Required Domestic Savings in Government Debt

Assume that all of the foreign lending to a country is strictly
limited to only financing a trade deficit and only purchasing government
debt. Then, any government debt issued in excess of these foreign
purchases would have to be purchased by domestic savers. This
remaining government debt that domestic savers would have to purchase

is defined as the Required Domestic Savings in Government Debt and is simply defined for our purposes as the difference between the total U.S. government budget deficit and the U.S. trade deficit (if any). Even if we relax our assumptions about foreign lending, this difference reflects a required domestic savings amount.

Figure 6 illustrates the Required Domestic Savings in Government Debt and the amount that the domestic banking system purchased since 1950. The peaks in Required Domestic Savings show that in times of recession the U.S. government stimulates the economy and runs budget deficits larger than trade deficits. If the domestic banking system does not purchase the government debt, then U.S. households and businesses must directly purchase the debt. Therefore, the gap between the Required Domestic Savings and the Banking System Purchases reflect the remaining amount of government debt that must be purchased by U.S. household and business savings.

Sometimes the gap becomes so large that it is dangerous to rely on private sector savings if a government wants to avoid a recession or depression. The gap in the early 1990s due to the S&L crisis is a case in point. The U.S. suffered a recession as the private sector was required to save almost 4% of GDP in order to pay for the cleanup of the S&L crisis.

After the financial crisis of 2008, the gap between the required domestic savings and the banking system purchases approached 8% of GDP. The interest rate required for the banking system to buy this debt would have been too high and would have caused a depression. Without bank purchases, the gap would have required U.S. households to save almost 8% of GDP in order to lend to the government. Instead, the Federal Reserve stepped in with quantitative easing so that interest rates could remain low, banks didn't have to buy the debt, and the U.S. consumer could continue to spend.

The trade deficit played a key role in motivating the U.S. government and the Federal Reserve to promote low interest rates and mortgage debt growth financed by Fannie Mae and Freddie Mac which led to a housing bubble (Figure 1). When the housing bubble blew up, the government along with the Federal Reserve had to step in with large budget deficits and quantitative easing to clean up the mess, maintain profits, and avoid a depression.

The Limits of Sector Debt

When trade deficits induce countries to compensate for lost profits with additional household and government debt, it typically raises the debt as a percent of GDP for both the household and government sector pushing them closer to their debt limit. Conversely, if a country running a trade deficit wants to avoid a rising debt to GDP ratio, it must allow profits to be taken from its economy with the associated economic consequences of a recession and political consequences of discontent and divisiveness.

Reinhardt and Rogoff (Reinhart & Rogoff, This Time is Different, 2011) have shown that when government net debt approaches 100% of GDP, growth tends to slow. While there is no exact limit for any country there is a point at which governments lose credibility with the market, interest rates rise, and capital flight begins.

It seems that 100% of GDP acts like a limit not only for governments but also for households and business. When the mortgage debt of U.S. households approached 100% of GDP, the bubble collapsed. When corporate debt has approached 100% of GDP historically, bankruptcies have accelerated.

The debt limit of a country is not so much the sum of the three sector's debt limits (household, business, government) as it is the maximum of the three sector's debt limits. When one of the three sectors approaches 100% of GDP, bad things tend to happen.

To maintain stability, countries should recognize these limits to debt and adopt policies to insure an adequate buffer is in place. Perhaps an allocation of debt equal to 60% of GDP for each sector is sustainable. We will explore this topic further in Chapter 5.

The Next Financial Crisis

An economy should rely on all three of its sectors to create profits. These three sectors are the household, business, and government sectors. Figure 7 and Figure 8 show how each sector, along with the trade deficit, has contributed to the source of profits since 1980. In both charts, profits are expressed as a percent of GDP.

The stacked bar chart in Figure 7 represents the contributions to profits from the household, business, and government sectors. The Total line represents the total amount of U.S. corporate after-tax profits and is equal to the sum of these three sector components and the trade deficit. The reason that the total line is below the stacked bars is because the U.S. has consistently run trade deficits which takes away an economy's profits.

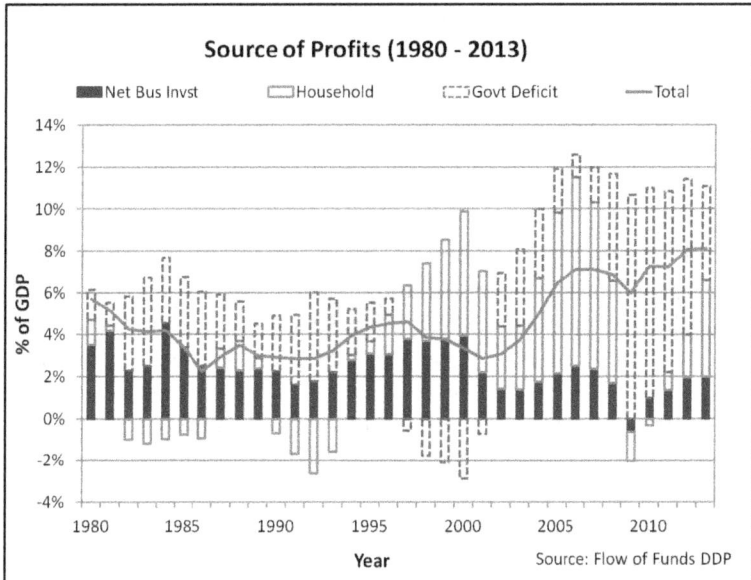

Figure 7: Stacked Sector Contributions of Profits

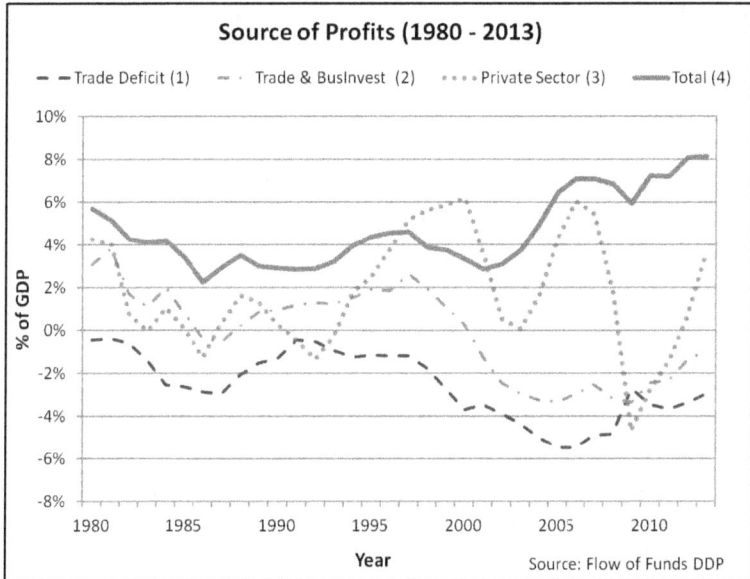

Figure 8: Cumulative Sector Contributions of Profits

Figure 8 uses the exact same data to illustrate the economic roller-coaster that the U.S. is experiencing. The first line at the bottom of

Figure 8 shows how the U.S. trade deficit has taken away U.S. corporate after-tax profits reaching a trough of almost -6% in 2006. The second line, Trade & BusInvst, now adds business investment to the trade deficit and shows how business investment has not been able to offset the trade deficit and the sum has been negative since 2000 leaving the household and government sectors' contributions as the only source of profits for the U.S. economy. The third line, Private Sector, now includes the household sector's contribution and shows how starting in the early 1990s the private sector's contribution has been on a roller-coaster with bubbles followed by busts. The Private Sector for this purpose is defined as the sum of the trade deficit, business, and household contributions. Finally, the Total line includes the government's contribution and shows the total corporate after-tax profits in the U.S. economy as a percent of GDP.

Figure 7 and Figure 8 illustrate how the government has stepped in with stimulus spending to offset the violent roller-coaster of the private sector's contributions. They also illustrate how the U.S. economy has gone from a three-legged stool with each sector, household, business, and government creating profits to essentially a one-legged stool. For the U.S. government to run a small budget deficit requires a business investment bubble like the technology bubble of the late 1990s or a housing bubble like 2003-2007 to overcome the lost profits from the trade deficit. As we should know by now, bubbles are not stable and very difficult to control.

In addition, Figure 7 and Figure 8 show that the level of profits in 2013 is not sustainable. Instead of targeting sustainable after-tax profits of 5% of GDP, profits in 2013 were above 8% of GDP. At some point in the future there will be a sudden or gradual 40% reduction in profits as a percent of GDP as they decline from 8% of GDP to a more sustainable 5% of GDP. Why an after-tax profit level of 5% of GDP is sustainable will be examined in Chapter 4.

If the U.S. continues down the road to economic turmoil, it will have to continue generating excess debt growth in order to replace the profits lost from the trade deficit. This means the U.S. government will have to run large budget deficits if it does not want to induce another housing bubble or commercial real estate bubble. Gradually, the net government debt outstanding will surpass 100% of GDP and the private sector will eventually lose confidence in the U.S. dollar.

Alternatively, perhaps the U.S. embarks on another housing bubble since nothing has really changed since the last crisis. There are still government guarantees in place with very little down payment required.

If another housing bubble bursts, the government will once again have to stimulate the economy with more quantitative easing by the Federal Reserve. In this scenario as well, the government debt to GDP ratio will rise and eventually the private sector will lose confidence in the U.S. dollar.

A government austerity scenario would reduce the government's budget deficit and leave it up to the private sector to replace the profits lost from the trade deficit. In this case, profits would eventually plummet and the U.S. would enter a deflationary depression with inadequate profits to stimulate investment and employment.

The most likely scenario if trade is not balanced is that both government and households continue to build up excessive debt until <u>domestic</u> confidence is lost in the U.S. dollar. Once U.S. households and businesses lose confidence in their own currency, the government must restore it by raising interest rates significantly to earn their trust back or impose capital controls. The lost confidence can take the form of rising inflationary demands or capital flight out of the currency. Once rates are raised, the debt servicing costs spiral higher and austerity must be imposed on U.S. taxpayers.

Once austerity is imposed to restore balance, it is virtually impossible to avoid a severe recession or depression. Abrupt changes in policy always lead to economic turmoil and unintended consequences. Tax policy becomes authoritarian and tries to punish those who benefitted from the previous policies. The poor suffer without adequate resources. Employment becomes difficult as the risk and uncertainty become too high. Meanwhile, foreign lenders who manipulated their currency receive additional compensation from higher interest rates. This compensation is almost like making reparation payments similar to how Germany had to make payments to foreign governments after World War I.

A policy that ignores the U.S. trade deficit will eventually require the U.S. to impose austerity on its citizens unless there is a transition to balanced trade. This transition needs to occur before the household, business, or government sector approach their debt limits of around 100% of GDP.

Two Paths to Follow

To return to balanced trade there are two paths that can be followed. One path is to devalue your currency faster than any other country by printing money. The other path is to restore cooperation amongst nations without punishing trade.

The race to print money is accomplished by government issuing debt combined with central bank purchases of the debt which is referred to as monetization. After the financial crisis of 2008, the quantitative easing of the Federal Reserve lowered U.S. interest rates and weakened the U.S. dollar. Japan has adopted quantitative easing as well but on a scale almost four times larger. Meanwhile, the European Union threatens quantitative easing if it can be properly structured. China claims to have "expanded the range of the yuan" but in reality has attempted to devalue along with the U.S. dollar.

With a weaker currency, exports become cheaper and imports become more expensive. Thus, a weaker currency tends to boost exports, reduce imports, and lowers trade deficits. However, there is nothing stopping any other country from printing money and devaluing their currency too. It becomes a race based on which country can devalue the most without losing the confidence of their citizens. The most authoritarian governments usually win this race.

The other path is to restore cooperation amongst nations by using incentives and the science of game theory. In game theory, deviations from balanced trade need to be punished so that countries return to balanced trade in their own self-interest. To hope for balanced trade when the current rules of the game are set up to encourage imbalances is irrational.

There is a policy that can be adopted to encourage balanced trade without punishing trade. Chapter 7 will discuss the current rules of the game and suggest a policy based on game theory to restore cooperation amongst nations that is sustainable.

Chapter 2 – Where Do Profits Come From?

When interviewing college graduates applying for jobs on Wall Street, I would ask them "If I added up all the profits in our economy, where do these profits come from?" Directing them away from a definition, like profit is the difference between revenue and costs, I was trying to determine the extent of their economic knowledge and whether they understood economics or memorized economics.

Without a proper framework, this question can be puzzling. The answers typically received ranged from improving products and beating the competition to entrepreneurship. However, these answers pertained to raising the standard of living of a country while I was interested in the macroeconomic source of profits and how policy decisions affect the amount of profits in an economy. It seems that we teach macroeconomics to students without adequately explaining one of its most important questions; where do profits come from?

Over the last 25 years, the symptoms of a poorly managed economy have become more prevalent. The U.S. economy has witnessed multiple financial bubbles, a destructive financial crisis, and a middle class struggling to keep up. The entire global economy has witnessed rising income disparity. There is also a misunderstanding within the financial industry and political community about whether debt growth is important or not and if so, what kind of debt growth.

These economic problems require a proper diagnosis. By understanding where profits come from, policymakers can propose effective solutions, avoid depressions, optimize sustainable growth, and identify bubbles before they cause economic damage and unnecessary hardship. At a more personal level, people interested in economics, government policy, or the stock market can identify the sources and magnitude of our problems and then advocate for change. This is the motivation for writing this book. Let's begin our journey down the road to economic prosperity.

The Profit Frame

The conventional world view analyzes economic policy through GDP (Gross Domestic Product) and National Income frames. In decision-making, the way a problem is studied is called a decision frame (Russo & Schoemaker, 1989). By looking through a frame, you may see a particular situation from an angle that might be different from others. Several frames can be used to diagnose a problem. Using multiple frames may expose biases, help isolate problems, and improve decisions. In surveys that frame questions, the answers you get may depend on how the question was asked and which frame was used. "Do you oppose A" may get a different result than "Do you support B".

An economy's GDP or National Income can be thought of as an upside-down pyramid balancing on its tip of profits.

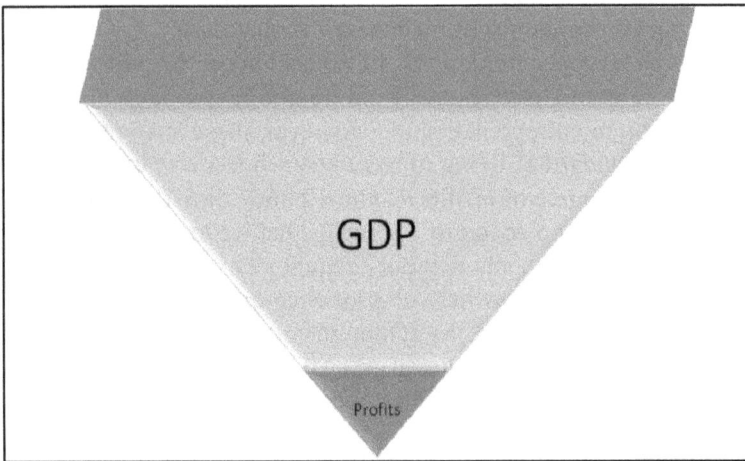

Figure 9 : GDP Balancing on Profits

Profits balance an economy and support the GDP above. Companies are created to make a profit. Even non-profit companies invest in for-profit companies so they can extend the duration of their chosen mission. If all of the profits in the U.S. economy were to disappear, the motivation for creating GDP would be greatly diminished. Why take the risk of starting a business and employing people if profits aren't available. Without profits in our current economic system, the

GDP pyramid would start to crumble and bring about an economic depression.

When citizens, businesses, or governments analyze policy decisions, looking through the profit frame as well as the GDP and National Income frames can provide an additional view of the situation and identify some hidden consequences of these decisions.

A Simple Example to Start

When faced with a difficult question, often simplifying a problem helps gain a better understanding. In this case, think of an economy of only two people in the world, the employee and the employer, making only one product. The employer has the money or capital and the employee is the only worker and consumer. If the employee doesn't buy the product, the product is not used and becomes worthless.

Assume the employee is paid $90 to manufacture the only product produced that represents the entire GDP of this two-person economy. The employer would like to sell the product for $100 to the employee and make a profit of $10. But how can the employee buy the product for $100 when they were only paid $90 to make it? This appears to be a conundrum, a chicken and egg dilemma.

Debt growth is one way of creating profits. If the employee borrowed $10 from the employer with the promise to pay it back later, the employee could buy the product for $100 and the employer would declare a $10 profit. The following year, the employee and the employer would be in the same situation. Again, the employee could borrow another $10, adding to their debt, and purchase the product. Each year the debt outstanding would grow. It may seem strange and counterintuitive that the more an individual borrows the greater the profits. However, as we will discover later, this debt must be financed by business, either directly or through the banking system, and used to purchase a domestic product or service.

Dividend Recycling is another way of creating profits. If the employee received a $10 dividend from the employer for some reason, then the employee could use the additional $10 of dividend income together with the $90 in wages to purchase the product for $100. Each year, this $10 of dividend income could be recycled from the employer to the employee and then returned back to the employer as profit.

Standard of Living

A common misunderstanding about profits is that people think they come directly from productivity and standard of living increases. However, there are important differences between measuring profits and measuring standards of living.

The middle class in the U.S. might actually enjoy a better standard of living today than the kings and queens of Europe a few hundred years ago. The middle class probably travels more, eats better food, has better healthcare, and lives longer. The increase in the standard of living over the centuries is due to the efforts of people all over the world striving to make things better and applying newly acquired knowledge. Our ancestors had the Agricultural Revolution, moving from hunter-gatherers to farmers, and the Industrial Revolution, moving from farmers to urban dwellers. Today, we are living in the Information & Medical Technology Revolution.

When thinking about profits and a rising standard of living, the easiest way to distinguish them is to realize that standard of living increases come from human effort and innovation while profits are derived solely from an accounting equation.

Human Effort ➔ *Standard of Living Increases*

Accounting Equation ➔ *Profits*

When I asked students the question of "Where do profits come from?" most of the answers dealt with human effort and productivity, describing where an increasing standard of living comes from. Their answers referred to entrepreneurs or investors who start businesses with better, more productive ways of providing a service or manufacturing a product which allows them to take market share from competitors and earn a profit.

Profits do capture increases in standard of living to some degree which may explain why it's easy to overlook the differences between them. However, adding up the total profits in an economy includes more than just gains in productivity and the benefits of human effort.

It is possible to have zero total profits in a country and still improve its standard of living. In our simplified example, if the employee came up with a way to make twice as many products as the previous year, the standard of living would double. However, if the employee is reluctant to borrow money and is only willing to buy the entire set for the $90 in wages they were paid by the employer, the profits in the simplified example would be zero.

It is also possible to have large total profits without any increase in the standard of living of an economy. In our simplified example, if the following year the employee was willing to borrow a large amount of money to purchase the one product, the standard of living wouldn't change because only one product was still produced but the profits would depend on how much the employee was willing to borrow.

When trying to keep score of how well a country is doing, looking at profits can be misleading. Large total profits in an economy may reflect excessive debt growth rather than productivity gains. Similarly, small profits due to an economy's unwillingness to borrow may mask the amount of progress that is being made in an economy's standard of living. Under any scenario, however, profits are very important because they motivate human effort and risk-taking which are key ingredients to a rising standard of living. Understanding the composition and sources of profits provides a unique insight into the overall health of an economy.

The Profit Equation

In our simplified example, there were only two people in the world. In the real world there are billions of people. Each person interacts with other people in a very complex network of transactions. However, the source of profits is still basically debt growth and dividend recycling.

In our simplified example, it was easy to identify the exact link of whose debt created the employers profit. In the real world, the links are all interconnected so one person's debt growth may show up somewhere else in the economy as another business' profit. If Mr. Jones borrows money to buy a product from Mr. Smith, it doesn't mean that Mr. Smith will make a profit. Mr. Smith will have to compete in the marketplace to make a profit. What can be said, however, is that the money Mr. Jones borrowed from the business sector was added to the pool of profits available in the economy and that the marketplace will allocate these profits some way through the billions of decisions and transactions made on a daily basis.

Michal Kalecki, a Polish economist and contemporary of John Maynard Keynes, derived the profit equation for a modern economy by using national accounting and dividing the economy into two groups, the Worker and the Capitalist. He derived the profit equation by using an accounting identity between national income and national output (GDP) illustrated in Table 1 (Kalecki, Selected essays on the dynamics of the capitalist economy, 1971).

Table 1 : A Simple Profit Equation

Category	National Income	=	National Output
Business [Capitalist]	+ Profits		+Gross Investment - Depreciation
Consumer [Worker]	+Worker's Wages		+ Worker's Consumption

Profits + Worker's Wages = Gross Investment -Depreciation + Worker's Consumption

The middle column of Table 1 lists the national income categories and states that National Income equals the sum of profits plus all wages received in an economy. This total reflects the income received to produce the GDP. In this simple profit equation, if Worker's Wages equals 95% of GDP, then Profits must equal 5% of GDP.

The right column of Table 1 lists the national output (GDP) categories. The national output column states that the GDP, or the value of the goods produced, equals the sum of net business investment (Gross Investment – Depreciation) plus household spending (Worker's Consumption). This total reflects the value of what was produced in the economy.

To understand the difference between the Gross Investment and Depreciation categories, consider how a refrigerator, which lasts several years, would be accounted for in Table 1. A refrigerator is produced in one year and is used for several years. In the year it is produced, its value would be included in Gross Investment. However, for the remaining useful life of the refrigerator, its value would gradually decline to reflect decay and use. In accounting, long-lived assets are depreciated as they get older to reflect this gradual consumption (decay) of the asset. This depreciation is sometimes referred to as Capital Consumption.

When Gross Investment and Depreciation are combined, it is referred to as Net Investment. Net Investment reflects how much additional output or value has been created and "stored" for future consumption.

Worker's Consumption is GDP output that is consumed in the same year that it is produced. We account for its production and value since a worker was paid wages to produce it. But at the end of the year, it is accounted for as being fully used or consumed in this simple profit equation.

If Depreciation were moved to the middle column in Table 1, Wages plus Depreciation would reflect something like business costs while Worker's Consumption plus Gross Investment remaining in the right column would reflect something like business revenue plus property, plant, and equipment investment plus inventory changes.

From Table 1, it is difficult to see how debt growth and dividend recycling play a role in the profit equation. A portion of debt growth is hidden inside Gross Investment when businesses or consumers borrow money to produce a capital good that hasn't depreciated yet. Dividend recycling and a portion of debt growth are also hidden in Worker's Consumption to the extent it exceeds Worker's Wages.

Adding more detail to Table 1 by creating additional groups for Government and Foreign Trade leads to two additional rows and the impact of taxes and trade. Notice that in Table 2 we now subtract Imports so only spending on domestic goods and services can generate profits.

Table 2: The Profit Equation with Government and Trade

Category	National Income =	National Output
Business	+ After-Tax Profits	+ Gross Investment - Depreciation
Consumer	+ After-Tax Wages	+ Worker's Consumption
Government	+ Tax Revenue	+ Government Spending
Trade		+ (Exports – Imports)

The last step is to define the categories of savings or borrowing for consumers, government, and foreign counterparts as illustrated in Table 3. Note that dividend recycling is now a part of Worker's Savings since it is hidden inside Worker's Consumption. We could have redefined Worker's Consumption to exclude dividend recycling and then

added an additional term for Dividend Recycling but instead have chosen
to just make a note of it.

Table 3: Definitions of Savings and Borrowing Categories

Savings Category	Definition
Net Investment	+ Gross Investment - Depreciation
Worker's Savings	+After-Tax Wages – Worker's Consumption
Government Deficits	+ Government Spending – Tax Revenue
Trade Deficits	+ Imports – Exports

Substituting these definitions into the profit equation of Table 2 leads to
the Profit Equation with Government, Trade, and Savings as seen in
Table 4 (Kalecki, 1972).

Table 4 : The Profit Equation with Government, Trade, and Savings

Category	Business Profits =	Sources of Profits
Business	+ After-Tax Profits	+ Net Investment
Consumer		– Worker's Savings
Government		+ Government Deficit
Trade		– Trade Deficit

After-Tax Profits = Net Investment – Worker's Savings + Government Deficit -Trade Deficit

It should now be easier to see from the Profit Equation in Table 4
that debt growth is an important source of profits. All of the items in the
right column of Table 4 are related to saving and borrowing.
Similar to how debt was hidden in Table 1, it is now portions of
GDP that are hidden in Table 4. Government Spending is hidden inside

the Government Deficit category and Worker's Consumption is hidden inside the Worker's Savings category.

To understand where profits come from, it is very useful to divide the sources of profits into the four categories in the left-hand column of the profit equation in Table 4.

- Business
- Consumer
- Government
- Trade

Before providing more clarity with examples, the five sources of financing (lending) available to the profit equation must be introduced. For every borrower there must be a lender.

Vendor Financing and Bank Credit

There are five sources of financing (lending) available to the profit equation.

- Vendor Financing
- Dividend Recycling
- Bank Credit (Money Multiplier Effect)
- Central Bank Monetization
- Official Foreign Reserves/Foreign Lending

Vendor financing refers to when a business lends money to its customer so the customer can buy a product or service of the business. Have you ever bought anything on layaway? If so, you participated in vendor financing. If the customer is eventually unable to pay, the business is not paid for the product or service provided. In our simplified example, the employer lending to the employee was an example of vendor financing. Vendor Financing typically finances about 10% of profits.

Dividend Recycling is similar to Vending Financing in that the business sector transfers money to the household sector in the form of dividend income. However, when the household sector spends the dividend income in the domestic economy, the money returns to the business sector and can be recycled again. Dividend Recycling is the only source of financing profits that does not depend on debt growth. Note that because it must be recycled back to the household sector, it cannot be locked up and used to finance business net investment. Dividend Recycling typically finances about 20% to 30% of profits.

If the household sector decides to liquidate savings from a previous year and decrease Worker's Savings, this also "finances" profits. For our purposes this is also classified as Dividend Recycling because it does not involve debt growth. However, households tend to build savings and therefore not "finance" profits from previous years' savings.

Interestingly, Dividend Recycling also plays a role in the long-term expected return of stock market indices. The long-term expected return of stock market indices equals the growth rate in nominal GDP plus Dividend Recycling expressed as a percent of GDP. However, the long-term growth rates in total stock market capitalizations do not benefit from Dividend Recycling and must grow at the same long-term rate as nominal GDP.

Bank Credit (Money Multiplier Effect) represents the loans that have been originated by the banking system using the money multiplier effect (Assets and Liabilities of Commercial Banks in the United States , 2012) and it plays a vital role in the creation of debt growth and profits. Since most businesses are not experts on the creditworthiness of their customers, banks typically provide this service to the economy. It is similar to Vendor Financing except the bank is the middleman and the banking system can "print money" from the money multiplier effect.

When 1) a bank lends to a customer, 2) the money is withdrawn from the banking system and given to a business in exchange for a product or service, and 3) the business deposits the money back into the banking system, these three combined transactions are equivalent to vendor financing. Instead of the business having an Accounts Receivable asset, it has a Bank Deposit asset while the customer has borrowed from a bank rather than from the business. The business sector must acquire the bank deposits from either the consumer or government sector for profits to be created.

As we will discover in the next chapter, Bank Credit benefits from the money multiplier effect. Because of the money multiplier effect, the banking system can print money to generate profits from debt growth. If the banking system were not able to print money from the money multiplier effect, then only Central Bank Monetization could print money. Bank Credit using the money multiplier effect typically finances about 60% of profits.

Central Bank Monetization can be viewed as a special case of Bank Credit where a central bank like the Federal Reserve can simultaneously create bank assets (reserves) and bank liabilities (bank deposits) simply by purchasing something. These central bank purchases are equivalent to bank lending in terms of their potential to generate profits if the bank deposits are eventually transferred to the business sector through the purchase of a domestic product or service. The central bank doesn't need the money multiplier effect to print money since it creates money when it settles the purchase. Central Bank Monetization typically finances about 5% of profits but it can be much larger as is the case with quantitative easing.

Official Foreign Reserves/Foreign Lending consists of loans made by foreign central banks and foreign private lenders. These loans are used to finance only the trade portion of the profit equation. In recent years, foreign central bank lending has been much larger than foreign private lending due to private sector limits on credit and foreign exchange risk.

Examples using the Profit Equation

To facilitate understanding of the profit equation, ten examples are provided to illustrate how they impact the categories and values in the right-hand column of the profit equation in Table 4 assuming all else is unchanged. The importance of debt growth used to purchase goods or services included in GDP is recurrent.

Example 1: A Consumer borrows from a bank to purchase a domestic product

When a consumer borrows from a bank to purchase a domestic product, this is accounted for as minus Worker's Savings and creates profit. In Table 4, Worker's Savings reflects changes in the Worker's net worth due to spending on domestic goods included in the Gross Domestic Product (GDP) of the country.

Since the consumer purchased a domestic product, the Trade Deficit did not change. The consumer must purchase something that was included in the GDP of the country in order to generate domestic profits from a reduction in Worker's Savings.

This example uses the money multiplier effect of the banking system to "print money" and finance the profits. If another household increased Worker's Savings by depositing money in a bank and the bank subsequently used this deposit as its source of money, the combined household savings and borrowing would offset in Worker's Savings and cancel any profits.

Example 2: A Consumer borrows from a bank to purchase a financial asset

If a consumer borrows money from the banking system to buy a financial asset, both the consumer's debt and financial asset would be categorized within Worker's Savings and cancel each other without a net change to any of the items in Table 4. By borrowing money from the banking system to buy a financial asset, a person is increasing their financial risk but they are not creating profits in the economy.

However, the seller of the financial asset would now have a bank deposit and may eventually spend the proceeds in the domestic economy and create profits. Sometimes one person's willingness to take on more financial risk results in another person using their additional Worker's Savings to increase spending and create profits. This is part of what is called the "wealth effect".

Example 3: U.S. Federal Government borrows from the Household Sector to fund Government Spending

Profits are not created when the federal government issues U.S. Treasury debt that is purchased by the household sector because the increase in the Government Deficit offsets or cancels the increase in Worker's Savings.

Like Example 1, profits are increased if the government borrows money to spend on domestic goods included in the GDP. This government spending would be accounted for as an increase in the Government Deficit category of Table 4. However, Worker's Savings also increases which cancels out the profits that the government spending created. The net result is the same as if the household had just spent the money themselves rather than lending it to the government to spend.

Similarly, the burden of government interest payments doesn't affect profits unless the business sector holds the debt. Government borrowing from households to make the interest payments cancel out in the profit equation. It is essentially like a circular flow with the money ending up where it started. However, the interest rate required to overcome the credit risk and induce this circular flow of money may increase and thus raise debt levels and slow economic growth.

Example 4: A Consumer buys a foreign product from wage income

When a consumer buys a foreign product from wage income, the Worker's Savings category is not affected because the after-tax Wage Income and the domestic portion of Worker's Consumption haven't changed.

The Trade Deficit category, however, increases and this lowers profits in the economy because domestic wage income was used to buy a foreign product rather than a domestic product.

Example 5: A Business borrows from a bank to build a domestic factory

Like Example 1, when a business borrows money from a bank to purchase products that are included in the GDP, profits are created. The business spending on a domestic factory would be categorized as an increase in Net Investment in Table 4.

This example also uses the money multiplier effect of the banking system to "print money" and finance the profits. If a household increased Worker's Savings by depositing money in the bank and the bank subsequently used this deposit as its source of money, the business spending on a domestic factory would be cancelled by the increase in Worker's Savings.

Example 6: A Consumer borrows from a bank to purchase an existing home

For the home buyer, the mortgage and the value of the existing home would both be categorized as Worker's Savings and cancel each other without a net change to any of the items in Table 4.

However, like Example 2, the amount of profits eventually created in the economy depends on how the proceeds of the home sale are used by the seller. Because home prices typically rise and homeowners make monthly mortgage payments, the mortgage of the new buyer is usually larger than the previous mortgage of the seller. As a result, an increase in the outstanding balance of all home mortgages in a country is mostly money that has been created in the banking system and can be spent in the domestic economy to create profits, whether to renovate a home or spend on other domestic goods or services.

This example also uses the money multiplier effect of the banking system to finance profits.

Example 7: A Corporation borrows from a bank in order to buy back its stock

If a corporation borrows money from a bank to buy back its stock it does not create profits. The buyback only reflects a change in the ownership structure of the company. Equity in the company is just being replaced with debt. Shareholders would exchange their stock in the company for bank deposits to reflect the sale of their shares.

For an individual shareholder, the form of Worker's Savings would change from equity to bank deposits but the amount of savings would not change. Since nothing tangible that is included in the GDP will have been purchased with the corporation's debt, it would not add to the pool of available profits for the economy.

However, if the shareholders who sold their stock to the corporation eventually use their bank deposit proceeds to purchase goods or services included in the GDP, profits are created by reducing Worker's Savings. Stock buybacks do play a role in spending due to the "wealth effect".

Example 8: Government Deficits compensating for Trade Deficits

In Table 4 government budget deficits increase profits while trade deficits decrease profits. Together, they cancel each other in the profit equation. It is typical for a country running a trade deficit to compensate for lost profits by running government budget deficits.

One benefit of adopting this policy for a government is that by running trade deficits, the government can justify a greater role for itself in an economy. On the other hand, this policy relies on the ability of the country (primarily the government) to borrow from foreign lenders. When a government loses market confidence, it must then rely on its own central bank to take the place of these foreign lenders or raise taxes during a financial crisis.

Example 9: The Financial Sector's Debt

The financial sector's debt is not included nor categorized in Table 4 to avoid double counting. Financial companies are just intermediaries, or middlemen. A bank is like a network hub where the borrower and the saver do not know each other but they both know the bank. While the financial sector may have a say in who is allocated money to spend in the real economy, it is the eventual borrower who spends the loan proceeds on products or services included in the GDP that is creating profits.

Excluding the financial sector's debt to avoid double counting does not mean the banking system is not important. The creation of bank credit is a vital ingredient in the creation of profits. Without bank credit and the money multiplier effect, it would be up to the central bank to finance the creation of profits.

Example 10: The Paradox of Thrift

If 1) the worker spends exactly the same amount as their after-tax wages on domestic made goods, 2) the trade deficit is zero, 3) the government spends exactly the same amount as their tax revenue, and 4) net investment by business is zero, then the sum of all the profits in the economy is zero. This is referred to as the paradox of thrift. Except for Dividend Recycling which comes from non-wage income or previous years' savings, somebody has to borrow from the banking system or business and then spend the proceeds in the domestic economy for profits to be created.

Categorizing Debt

Most macroeconomics textbooks describe GDP by segmenting the economy into distinct sectors such as Consumption (C), Investment (I), Government Spending (G), and a Trade Surplus (Ex – Im) (Samuelson & Nordhaus, 2005). By segmenting the economy this way, it is easier to diagnose how the economy is behaving and what actions or behaviors are responsible for GDP growth or contraction.

When looking through the profit frame as illustrated in the right column of Table 5 below, the data on debt growth is segmented into Consumer Debt (C_d), Business Investment Debt (I_d), Government Debt (G_d), and Foreign Debt (F_d).

Table 5: Categorizing GDP and Debt Growth

Category	GDP	Debt Growth
Formula	GDP = C+I+G+(Ex–Im)	Debt Growth $=C_d+I_d+G_d+F_d$
Consumer	Consumer Spending (C) Consumer Investment (I)	Consumer Debt (C_d)
Business	Business Investment (I)	Non-Financial Business Debt (I_d)
Government	Government Spending (G) Government Investment (G)	Government Debt (G_d)
Trade	Exports (Ex) – Imports (Im)	Foreign Debt (F_d)

Consumer Debt (C_d) is debt that is held by individuals. The largest debt that the American consumer has is a home mortgage. A mortgage is a loan that is provided by a bank or financial institution when a homeowner purchases a home. The home is collateral for the mortgage. If the homeowner doesn't pay the mortgage, the bank can foreclose, evict the homeowner, and sell the home to get back the money it lent to the homeowner. Credit card debt is another type of consumer debt. However, it is very small compared to mortgage debt because of a lack of collateral backing credit card debt. Recently, student loan debt is becoming a significant part of Consumer Debt. This is because the U.S. government plays a large role in guaranteeing student loans and takes the risk of the students not paying back the loan.

Non-Financial Business Debt (I_d) is primarily corporate debt. There are several kinds of corporate debt with different forms of collateral to protect the lender and lower the interest rate on the debt. Some corporate debt has equipment as collateral. Some corporate debt is called Senior meaning that in a bankruptcy, the lender will get paid first after the employees and suppliers and it may have the entire company as its collateral. Some corporate debt is not supported by collateral at all and just relies on the cash flows of the company to get paid back.

Small business (non-corporate) debt is similar to consumer debt in that it is primarily mortgage debt that is collateralized by the property, plant, or equipment that was purchased.

Government Debt (G_d) is federal, state, and local government debt. In the U.S., federal government debt is the largest portion of government debt. In most cases, government debt is not supported by collateral but relies on the taxing power of the government. State and local government debt have several different forms, some of which rely on collateral of a project and some of which rely on the taxing power of the state or local government.

Foreign Debt (F_d) is the net debt that foreign individuals, businesses, or governments lend to domestic borrowers to finance a trade deficit or current account deficit. The collateral supporting foreign debt depends on who is borrowing the money and the type of loan.

Summary

In this chapter we learned about the profit equation and how profits come from an accounting equation that is <u>primarily a function of debt growth</u>. We resolved a misunderstanding about profits by distinguished between profits and an increase in the standard of living of a country that is derived from productivity and human effort. We described the four categories of the profit equation

- Net Business Investment
- Worker's Savings
- Government Deficits
- Trade Deficits

and introduced the five sources of financing (lending) profits.

- Vendor Financing
- Dividend Recycling
- Bank Credit (Money Multiplier Effect)
- Central Bank Monetization
- Official Foreign Reserves/Foreign Lending

The difference between understanding economics and memorizing economics is the ability to see the "gears" of an economy. What is the current state of the economy? What economic gears or levers have moved? How does a certain action affect the economy directly and indirectly? Looking through the profit frame will provide a unique view of how the economy is functioning, how to control the growth of the economy, how to make wiser business and government policy decisions, and how to maintain a sustainable economy without bubbles or depressions.

Chapter 3 – The Business Cycle and Managing Debt Growth

This chapter continues to build a strong foundation for the profit frame by examining how profits and debt growth are linked to the business cycle and how the Federal Reserve sets reserve requirements, creates money, and uses interest rates to influence the rate of debt growth in the U.S. We will also examine the errors that the Federal Reserve made during the Great Depression and how the lessons learned were applied in the financial crisis of 2008.

The Business Cycle

History shows that economies move in cycles with periods of rising income, falling income, and occasional economic or financial collapses. There are many variables that can affect the business cycle. In fact, the business cycle was a motivating factor for Michal Kalecki to derive the profit equation.

In the past, long time lags between when a product was manufactured and when it was sold could lead to inventory buildups or shortages producing cycles of activity. Today, businesses use just-in-time inventory systems to mitigate the time lag and reduce this source of cyclicality in their business (Morgan D. P., 1991).

The business cycle is also affected by the herd-like behavior of individuals and decision makers. There is a Japanese proverb that says "The nail that sticks out gets hammered". The proverb implies to not deviate too far from what other people think or are doing.   Today there is a branch of economics called behavioral finance that tries to understand how decisions are made and what are some of the biases that are inherent in the human mind (Thaler, 1993). Game theory is another branch of economics that investigates cooperation and decisions in a game of rewards and threats (Myerson, 1991).

Yet with all the advancements in technology and information, economies still have business cycles as well as economic and financial collapses. In 2008, the U.S. suffered a financial crisis that was foreseeable through the profit frame. Since 2011, the European Union has struggled to avoid another economic crisis and have had to rely on bailouts and European Central Bank promises to avoid collapse. The link between profits and debt growth plays an important role in the business cycle.

Entrepreneurs and business people are usually looking for ways to increase profits and grow. It is natural for successful businesses to want to grow, by borrowing money or reinvesting their profits into the business for even larger future profits. It is usually when a business is very profitable that the owner aggressively wants to grow or finance their customers. It is much rarer for a business losing money to want to grow larger or finance their customers. Thus, when an economy's profits are high, everyone wants to invest for growth and debt growth increases. This debt growth can create additional profits for the economy in what is called a positive feedback loop. When the bad investments start rippling through the economy and people become more fearful, they reduce their investment and debt growth which lowers the amount of profits in the economy. Falling profits induce fear and an even greater slowdown in debt growth and profits. It is this positive feedback loop of debt growth and profits that plays a large role in the natural evolution of the business cycle. If the debt growth is unchecked and a particular sector reaches its debt limit at which market confidence is lost, financial crises typically occur along with economic collapses.

The Federal Reserve and Creating Money

In order to mitigate the positive feedback loop between debt growth, profits, and a boom-bust business cycle, governments try to regulate banking and credit (i.e., debt growth). In the U.S., the Federal Reserve (also known as "the Fed") is the central bank and is responsible for regulating large commercial banks and the creation of money. The Fed uses two primary tools, reserve requirements and interest rate policy, to control the level of debt growth and consequently the growth and cyclicality of the U.S. economy (Board of Governers of the Federal Reserve System, 2005) In times of financial crises, the Fed can also use quantitative easing to increase reserves above the minimum legal requirement to facilitate debt growth and profits.

Reserve requirements represent the amount of money a domestic commercial bank has to hold at a Federal Reserve Bank or in a bank's vault. The amount required is some percentage of the checking or demand deposits that a bank has acquired and is liable for. This percentage must not be lent out but rather held for safekeeping. The reserve requirement is used to control the amount of money in the banking system.

In 2012, the reserve requirement on bank deposits was 10%. This means that 10% of the relevant deposits in the U.S. banking system each week during 2012 had to be held in reserve. This is referred to as fractional-reserve banking. By only having to reserve 10% of these deposits, this allows the banking system to create or "print" money from the money multiplier effect (Samuelson & Nordhaus, 2005).

Table 6 provides an example of how a $100 bank reserve created by the Federal Reserve can create $1,000 of banking system deposits. This process is known as the money multiplier effect. Notice that while a single bank cannot create money, a group of banks (i.e., the banking system) can.

Table 6 : Example of How the Banking System Can Create Money

Deposits	Loans	Reserves
Bank A Receives $100	Bank A Loans $90	Bank A Reserves $10
Bank B Receives $90	Bank B Loans $81	Bank B Reserves $9
Bank C Receives $81	Bank C Loans $72.90	Bank C Reserves $8.10
…	…	…
Total Deposits $1000	Total Loans $900	Total Reserves $100

If the Federal Reserve wants to prevent banks from lending money without changing the interest rate in the economy, it can change the reserve requirement. Making banks hold a higher percentage of their deposits in reserves makes it more difficult for banks to lend if they lack the reserves needed to support their lending from the money multiplier effect.

Besides the banking system creating money from the multiplier effect, the Federal Reserve can also create bank deposits or "print" money. In Table 6, we started with a $100 bank reserve created by the Federal Reserve. How does the Fed create a bank reserve and bank deposit? They create a bank reserve (asset) and a bank deposit (liability) when they simply buy something.

Each day, the Fed buys and/or sells U.S. Treasuries or other safe government debt (Board of Governers of the Federal Reserve System, 2005). If the Fed only promises to lend or borrow the securities temporarily, the transaction is called a repo or reverse repo, respectively.

For example, when the Fed buys a U.S. Treasury Bill, the seller's bank is given cash or reserves by the Fed and the seller's bank account is credited with the proceeds. Essentially, the Fed creates a deposit into the seller's bank account by fiat. Because a bank deposit is a bank liability, the Fed also gives this bank an equal amount of cash or reserves at the Fed which is a bank asset. Then, the seller of the U.S. Treasury Bill can withdraw the cash to purchase a product or service. If the cash is saved, the bank can lend out a portion of this new bank deposit thus increasing debt growth and the money supply.

On the other hand, if the Fed sells a U.S. Treasury Bill from its inventory, then the buyer must purchase it with cash. In this case, both the reserve asset of the bank and the money in the buyer's bank account vanishes when the cash is transferred back to the Fed. With fewer reserves, the banking system may have to limit its lending.

The ability to create or "print" money either through the money multiplier effect or Federal Reserve purchases is vital to the creation of profits. The creation of money is what allows profits to be created without vendor financing. When the banking system is creating deposits through the multiplier effect by lending to government, business, or consumers, it means that the proceeds of these loans can be spent in the domestic economy to generate profits.

The Federal Reserve Board of Governors is also responsible for setting interest rate policy. They typically use the Fed Funds rate to do this (Board of Governers of the Federal Reserve System, 2005). This is the interest rate that banks pay to borrow reserves from other banks with excess reserves so all of the banks can meet their legal reserve requirement. So by controlling this interest rate, the Fed influences the amount of lending in the economy.

Before the financial crisis of 2008, the Federal Reserve did not pay interest on the reserves that banks held at the Federal Reserve. As a result, if the Fed wanted to "enforce" its interest rate policy, it would have to target how much cash or reserves to give to the banks or take from the banks. Since the financial crisis of 2008, the Federal Reserve has begun paying interest on reserves so now to "enforce" the Fed Funds rate they have an additional tool by changing the interest rate they pay on reserves.

By setting reserve requirements and interest rates on bank reserves, the Federal Reserve has the power to control the amount of debt growth in the U.S. economy and counter the positive feedback loop that debt growth has on the business cycle.

The Federal Reserve's errors during the Great Depressions are an instructive lesson on the importance of debt growth, bank credit, and Federal Reserve policy.

The Great Depression

The Federal Reserve played a large role in deepening the Great Depression although it was unintentional (Friedman & Schwartz, A Monetary History of the United States, 1867-1960, 1963). After the stock market crash of 1929, the bad loans of the boom were uncovered and some banks in the U.S. had to report their losses and sometimes their insolvency. When bank depositors discovered that their bank had inadequate capital or liquidity and they could be restricted from withdrawing their money or lose a portion of their deposits if they were too late, they would go to the bank and demand their money immediately and the contagion would cause a run on the bank.

Bank managers and their stockholders wanted to avoid a run on their bank. So with a bad economy and contagious rumors, banks decided that it would be prudent to hold some excess cash in their vault or excess reserves at the Federal Reserve. The banks could use the excess cash or reserves to satisfy their depositors in a panic and thus avoid a liquidity squeeze. Without excess reserves, the banks could have borrowed from the Federal Reserve but they were reluctant to do so because it implied weakness and increased the threat of panic.

Unfortunately, the Federal Reserve thought that a bank's legal reserve requirement was also its desired level of reserves. The Fed believed that if the banks needed money they could borrow it from the Fed. The Fed didn't appreciate the reluctance banks had to show any sign of weakness by borrowing from the Fed. The Fed also discouraged continuous borrowing from its discount window. So, although the public and the banks wanted more cash and reserves, the misunderstanding resulted in the Fed keeping the level of reserves and cash in circulation basically unchanged.

The Fed was also trying to defend the U.S. dollar against speculative currency attacks. Some foreign banks were converting their U.S. dollars into gold in case the dollar was later devalued in terms of gold. To counter this currency attack and induce holders of U.S. dollars not to convert to gold, the Fed raised interest rates and was reluctant to increase bank reserves above the legal requirement even though the amount of bank loans outstanding was shrinking.

Without the Fed supplying excess reserves, the banks were forced to sell assets and call in loans to raise cash. It was the money multiplier effect in reverse. This forced selling lowered the value of bank assets and bank capital. Then, the cash raised would be withdrawn by depositors fearful that their bank would be the next to fail. Without the desired level of reserves they needed, the banks were sitting ducks. Each time a bank run occurred, the hoarding of cash increased the probability of another bank run. Excess bank reserves were eventually created after the collapse of many banks but by then the damage to the global economy had already been done. Over a period of several years, the money supply shrank by over 30% (Figure 10)!

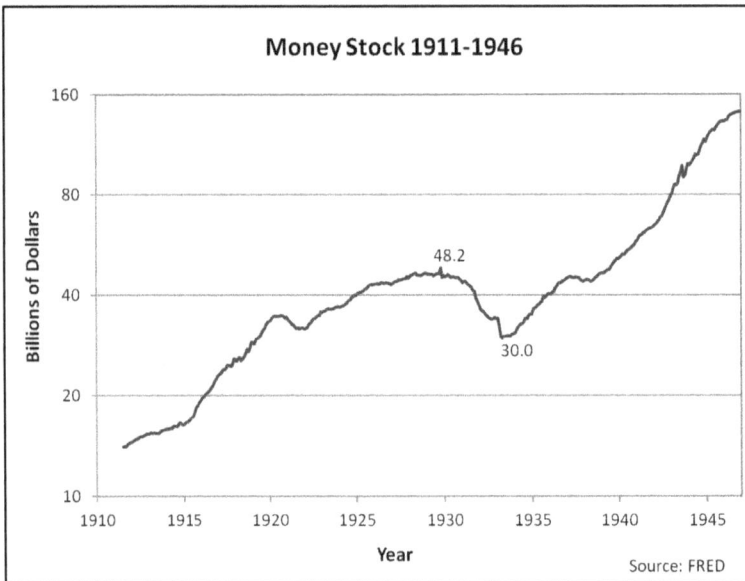

Figure 10 : Money Supply 1911-1946

In 2002, Ben Bernanke, a then member of the Board of Governors of the Federal Reserve System and student of the Great Depression, apologized for the actions of the Fed and promised that the Fed would never let it happen again (Bernanke, On Milton Friedman's Ninetieth Birthday, 2002).

2008 : Decoupling Banking Reserves & Interest Rates

In the prelude to the financial crisis of 2008, the U.S. Government and the Federal Reserve failed in their regulatory duties over banks (Friedman & Kraus, 2011). As will be examined later, they also allowed debt growth to become too large. It was only a matter of time before a crisis would occur and the economy would face a sudden collapse.

In 2008, when the collapse occurred and there was a risk of bank runs, the Federal Reserve didn't make the same mistakes as in the Great Depression and instead flooded the financial system with excess reserves (Kroszner & Melick, 2009). When a bank was determined to be insolvent, it was taken over by the FDIC, part of the U.S. government, and the good assets sold to another bank (Campbell, LaBrosse, Mayes, & Singh, 2007). By making sure there was enough money in the banking system as lender of last resort, as well as unlimited deposit insurance to satisfy the depositors (FDIC - Financial Institution Letters, 2008), the Fed and U.S. Treasury prevented the bank runs, reduction in lending, and forced selling of bank assets that devastated the economy during the Great Depression.

During the financial crisis of 2008 and the slow recovery afterwards, the Federal Reserved embarked on a policy of quantitative easing (Bernanke, The Crisis and the Policy Response, 2009). Under quantitative easing, the Federal Reserve creates more bank reserves than the banking system legally requires by purchasing large quantities of U.S. Treasuries or other securities which creates bank deposits and reserves.

In an important change after the financial crisis of 2008, the Federal Reserve decided to *decouple* the reserves requirements of the banking system and the Fed Funds interest rate target for the U.S. economy. The Federal Reserve now pays banks interest to hold their cash or reserves at the Federal Reserve (Monetary Policy IOR FAQ, 2012). In the past, if the Fed wanted to raise interest rates it might have had to take cash or reserves from the banks. This could reduce bank liquidity at a time when the banks might need more liquidity. Now, regardless of the amount of reserves in the banking system, the Federal Reserve just has to raise the interest rate it is willing to pay banks for the cash they hold at the Federal Reserve. This should make it easier for the Federal Reserve to control debt growth in the future using only interest rate policy after quantitative easing has created enormous excess reserves in the banking system.

Summary

In this chapter we have seen how the positive feedback loop of debt growth and profits affect the business cycle. We also discussed how the banking system creates money through the money multiplier effect and how the Federal Reserve is responsible for controlling debt growth by setting reserve requirements, the Fed Funds interest rate, and the interest rate they pay on reserves.

It is important for the Fed to keep debt growth on a sustainable, steady growth rate to avoid bubbles and depressions.

Chapter 4 – Understanding Money, Credit, & Inflation

This chapter will examine several different aspects of money and banking that will be useful in later chapters. These include

- What is money?
- The "credit supply" of securitizations and official foreign reserves.
- How collateral affects debt growth and profits.
- The pros and cons of quantitative easing.
- What causes inflation?
- The pitfalls of the gold standard.

After this chapter, we will be ready to understand how we arrived at our current economic malaise and what prescriptions are required.

Money & Credit

What is money? It is a financial instrument whose value is certain (stable), accessible, and easy to exchange for goods or services. Economists have different money supply measures depending on how they define certain and accessible. Bank deposits are important because of their promise to be accessible with a certain value.

The demand for certainty and access to money varies with the season and with risk tolerances. The Federal Reserve was established to provide flexibility to the supply of money to match the seasonal demands and be the lender of last resort.

Money is like a hot potato during bull markets. Somebody has to own money during the good times and everyone wants to own it in a crisis.   During a financial crisis, when trust disappears, the demand for money usually skyrockets due to its perceived certainty in value and accessibility.

While money is at the center of our financial system, credit can be just as important to an economy and profits. Credit can take the form of vendor financing, lending between households and/or government, and foreign lending. One way to think about money and credit is by representing them as a target in archery.

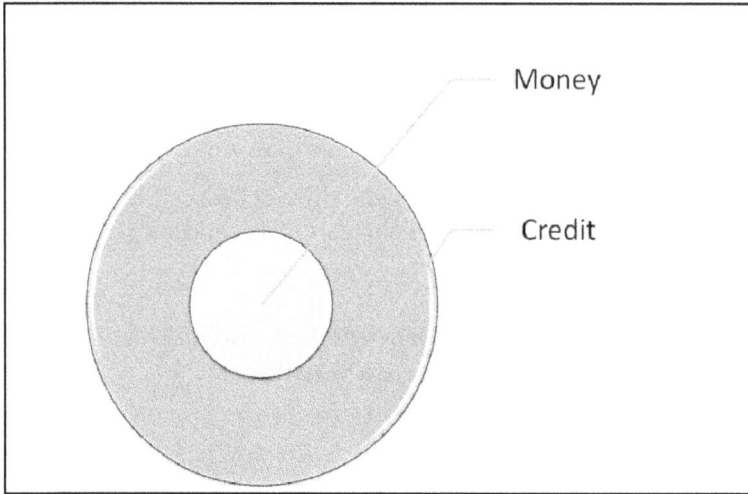

Figure 11 : The Monetary Target of Money and Credit

Our monetary target has a smaller circle representing money inside a larger circle representing credit. We want a monetary target with the right proportions to insure stability and a proper size relative to the economy to optimize growth. While investigating the proper size, economists came up with the notion of the velocity of money.

What is the velocity of money? Economists had two types of data, GDP and money supply, and wanted to write an equation linking one to the other. So they created a variable to represent the number of times that the money is spent to produce the GDP and write the following economic equation.

$$GDP = MoneySupply * Velocity$$

In reality, the velocity variable has little tangible value or robustness. There is a link between the money supply and GDP. It traverses from the money supply growth rate, which is a significant component of debt growth, to profits and then to GDP.

When the proportions between the credit supply and money supply change, the link between the money supply and GDP is weakened. The proportions vary depending on banking regulations, home values, trade deficits, trust in the financial system, bankruptcy, and investor sentiment.

Money will be defined for our purposes as cash and bank deposits. Cash is on the liability side of the Federal Reserve's balance sheet. Bank deposits are on the liability side of the commercial banks' balance sheets. This definition is also similar to what most economists would call money such as the M1 Money Supply (The Money Supply, 2012).

Credit will be defined for our purposes as any kind of non-financial sector debt that is not financed by bank deposits (i.e., not money). By defining credit in this way, we are identifying the sources of lending outside of the banking system which can affect debt growth, profits, and inflation. Credit is created when a saver lends to a borrower.

While savings cannot not "printed" like money, there are two important sources of savings in which significant amounts of credit can be created.

- Official Foreign Reserves
- Home Equity

Should official foreign reserves be considered money or credit? When a foreign central bank buys a U.S. dollar asset, they can print money in their own currency. In other words, they have the power to create a bank reserve and bank deposit in their own currency and then execute a foreign exchange trade to pay for the U.S. dollar asset. However, foreign central banks typically "sterilize" their U.S. dollar purchases. Sterilization refers to when a central bank sells a domestic asset in their portfolio to pay for the purchase of a foreign asset. In the end, a domestic asset acting as collateral backing the local currency will have been replaced with a foreign asset (Dominguez).

Whether foreign central banks sterilize their purchases or not, since their "lending" is not financed by the U.S. banking system or the Federal Reserve, it is classified as credit for our purposes. Foreign central banks play a large role in the "credit supply" of the U.S. A very large portion of U.S. government debt is held by the global central banks, not just the U.S. central bank.

Home Equity and securitized mortgages play a large role in the shadow banking system. Securitization involves moving a bank asset and bank liability into a non-bank entity like a money market or mutual fund. These non-bank entities are considered part of the shadow banking system. In terms of home equity, the process of securitization involves converting a mortgage loan into a security (e.g., mortgage-backed security) and converting a bank deposit into a mutual fund holding. Even though a bank deposit was essential at the beginning of the process, because it was converted to a mutual fund holding, it is considered part of the "credit supply" for our purposes.

When investors redeem their money from money market funds or mutual funds during panics such as the financial crisis of 2008, these funds are forced to sell their assets. Then, banks and the Federal Reserve, acting as the lender of last resort, are called upon to purchase the mutual fund assets being sold. If bank deposits are viewed as safer than money market funds or mutual funds, banks will simultaneously receive a large share of the proceeds from mutual fund redemptions as bank deposits.

Many of the regulations after the financial crisis of 2008 deal with regulating the shadow banking system. Regulators hope to avoid large, sudden changes in the "credit supply" by reducing the conflicts of interest on those creating the mortgage and asset-backed securities.

The Importance of Collateral

Most debt that is created requires collateral. Banks do not typically make unsecured loans. A mortgage is collateralized by the value of the house. For business loans, the equipment, building, patents, or other assets of the company are used as collateral. Only governments can borrow without collateral up to a limit.

In the financial crisis of 2008, increasing collateral requirements were a key factor in the deleveraging and forced selling that occurred (Adrian, Begalle, Copeland, & Martin, 2011). One day an asset was considered good collateral with a collateral value of $100 and the next day its collateral value was only worth $50. Without sufficient collateral, investors and speculators were forced to sell assets and reduce their leverage and debt.

If an economy is starved of collateral, it can be difficult to generate debt growth and profits. A service-based economy relies more on intangible assets like patents and information compared to an industrial economy that relies on tangible assets like property, plant, and equipment. As the U.S. and the world migrate to a larger service-based economy from an industrial, manufacturing-based economy, the amount of tangible collateral that can be used to generate debt growth may become an issue. There are currently worries about a "collateral crisis" that is holding back bank lending (Pagliery, 2012).

Banks may have to rely on new sources of collateral or take larger risks than they have had to in the past. They may have to make more loans based only on the cash flows of a business. Software is being developed to analyze a business's social media and business reputation (Small businesses turn to alternative lenders, 2012). American Express is offering loans based on a forecast of a business's revenue that utilizes an American Express card (Pagliery, 2012).

The U.S. government should place more importance on trade policy and the loss of tangible assets that can be used as collateral to generate sustainable debt growth and profits. Housing collateral cannot be the only source of collateral growth in an economy.

Quantitative Easing

In the aftermath of the 2008 financial crisis, the Federal Reserve embarked on several quantitative easing (QE) programs. Under quantitative easing, the Federal Reserve makes large-scale purchases of assets from the market injecting excess reserves (cash) and bank deposits into the banking system. The cash reserves are considered excess reserves because the subsequent total amount of reserves in the banking system is above the legal requirement.

The Fed's motivation for QE was to fill the gap between the amount the U.S. government wanted to borrow and the amount the private sector could save without causing a depression. The federal government's budget deficit needed to be financed from a combination of domestic lending, foreign lending, and quantitative easing.

Equation 1: The Quantitative Easing Gap

QE Gap = Federal Gov't Budget Deficit
*   – Domestic Non-Bank Lending to Federal Gov't*
*   – Domestic Bank Lending to Federal Gov't*
*   – Foreign Lending to Federal Gov't*

Typically, the Fed only supplies enough reserves to target interest rates and the quantitative easing required each year is close to 0.25% of GDP. The domestic private sector and banks must lend to the federal government for the quantitative easing amount to equal this. In the years immediately following the financial crisis of 2008, the Federal Reserve has filled the federal government's financing gap with its quantitative easing programs.

Table 7: Quantitative Easing Variables for 2011

Variable	Description	Estimate (% of GDP)
Federal Gov't Budget Deficit	Annual Budget Deficit of Federal Gov't	8.7%
State & Local Gov't Budget Deficit	Annual Budget Deficit of State and Local Gov't	2.1%
Net Investment	Private Sector Net Investment	3.0%
Worker's Savings	Financial Savings of Households, Non-Profits, and Non-Corporate Business	2.3%
Domestic Non-Bank Lending to Gov't	Net Amount of Government Debt Purchased by the Private Sector excluding Banks	0%
Bank Lending to Gov't	Net Amount of Government Debt Purchased by the Banking System	0%
Trade Deficit	Imports minus Exports	3.7%
Foreign Lending to Federal Gov't	Net Amount of Federal Government Debt Purchased by Foreign Lenders	≈ 3.7%

Table 7 provides an approximation to the U.S. economy in 2011 and the years after the financial crisis. In 2011, the U.S. federal government sector wanted to run a budget deficit of 8.7% of GDP (Federal Reserve Statistical Release, 2011). The Federal Reserve did not want the household or business sector to lend to the federal government because it would have led to a drop in consumption and possibly higher rates. Banks were also under pressure to raise capital. Interest rates would have had to rise significantly to induce banks to lend to the federal government. Finally, the U.S. trade deficit was 3.7% of GDP implying that net foreign lending would also approximate 3.7% of GDP so that the current account and capital account would offset each other

Using the data from Table 7 in Equation 1, the QE gap in 2011 equates to 5% of GDP or around $65 billion per month which approximates the monthly sizes of the QE programs.

Notice in Equation 1 that a large reduction in the quantitative easing gap comes from Foreign Lending to Federal Gov't. This is one of the reasons that the U.S. government doesn't confront the trade deficit. A willing foreign buyer of U.S. debt allows the U.S. government to increase its role in the economy. The trade deficit also puts pressure on the growth in U.S. wage income helping to contain inflation.

Suppose that the banking system financed the government budget deficit instead of the Federal Reserve's quantitative easing purchases. They could have done so with money creation but the banking system would have required higher long-term interest rates than the Federal Reserve desired. Banks typically own short-term government securities (Developing the Domestic Government Debt Market, 2007). Banks are reluctant to buy long-term government debt unless they can earn what is called positive carry. Positive carry means that the bank expects to receive a higher interest rate from its investments than it pays its depositors. Relying on the banking system to buy government debt is costly because of the interest rates required to be appealing to banks (Li, 2011).

Next, suppose that U.S. households financed the federal government budget deficit without a collapsing economy. What interest rate do you think the U.S. saver would have required? They would have had to give almost 5% of their income to the U.S. government? This would have been like a 5% of GDP tax hike. Without the ability to extract home equity to purchase U.S. government debt, in no time the U.S. government would have been staring at interest rates similar to Spain and Italy of 5% during the European crisis and the market would have been clamoring for the Federal Reserve to lower the credit spread on U.S. government debt through quantitative easing and fill the gap.

Finally, suppose that U.S. households financed the federal government budget deficit with a collapsing economy. In this case, households would have accepted low interest rates on U.S. government debt. However, without quantitative easing or the banking system's money multiplier effect, household savings and the trade deficit would have cancelled the government deficit in the profit equation. According to the profit equation, total profits would have dropped to the level of weak net private sector investment and would have devastated job creation and economic stability. The flight to safety would have become a self-fulfilling prophecy.

The quantitative easing programs of the Federal Reserve has allowed U.S. savers and banks to avoid having to finance the budget deficits of the U.S. government. Rather than waiting for credit spreads to rise or the economy to collapse, the Federal Reserve preempted any fallout. Quantitative easing creates profits if the government spending results in the purchase of domestic goods included in the GDP.

However, rather than targeting Domestic Non-Bank Lending to the Federal Government (i.e. household and/or business lending to the federal government), the Federal Reserve could have targeted sustainable profits. Since household lending to government is part of Worker's Savings in the profit equation, we can set Domestic Non-Bank Lending to the Federal Government equal to Worker's Savings minus State & Local Government Budget Deficits as a goal.

Equation 2: Set Worker's Savings Goal for Quantitative Easing Gap

$$\begin{array}{l} Domestic\ Non\text{-}Bank\ Lending \\ \qquad to\ Federal\ Gov't \end{array} = \begin{array}{l} +\ Workers\ Saving's \\ -\ State\ \&\ Local\ Gov't\ Deficits \end{array}$$

Then, we can rearrange the profit equation from Table 4 to express State & Local Government Budget Deficits minus Worker's Savings into the following.

Equation 3: Relate Domestic Non-Bank Lending to Profit Equation

$$\begin{array}{l} +\ State\ \&\ Local\ Gov't\ Deficits \\ \qquad -\ Workers\ Saving's \end{array} = \begin{array}{l} +\ After\text{-}Tax\ Profits \\ -\ Net\ Investment \\ +\ Trade\ Deficits \\ -\ Federal\ Gov't\ Budget\ Deficits \end{array}$$

After replacing negative Domestic Non-Bank Lending to Federal Gov't in Equation 1 with the right-hand side of Equation 3, the quantitative easing gap becomes a function of after-tax profits as illustrated in Equation 4.

Using 5% of GDP as a sustainable After-Tax Profit Target, the variables in Table 7 would have suggested a financing gap of 2.2% of GDP or $28 billion per month in 2011. At its peak in 2012, the QE policy of the Fed reached a level of $85 billion per month almost three times the level required to target sustainable profits. This difference inflated profits and pushed the stock market to record highs in an attempt to generate employment growth and unsustainable consumption.

Equation 4: Quantitative Easing Gap that Targets Profits

$$
\begin{aligned}
QE\ Gap = &\ After\text{-}Tax\ Profit\ Target \\
&- Net\ Investment \\
&- State\ \&\ Local\ Gov't\ Deficits \\
&+ Worker's\ Savings \\
&- Bank\ Lending\ to\ Federal\ Gov't \\
&+ Trade\ Deficit \\
&- Foreign\ Lending\ to\ Federal\ Gov't
\end{aligned}
$$

There is a downside to quantitative easing (QE). A bank deposit is a liability of a bank. Banks voluntarily create bank deposits when they create a loan that they believe is worth more than the deposit liability. Instead of a bank voluntarily creating a bank loan and bank deposit, quantitative easing forcibly creates bank deposits and gives the banks a Federal Reserve Note (cash) as an asset to offset the bank deposit liability. It is like monetary foie gras where the banks are the ducks or geese being force fed.

The first danger of quantitative easing is that the Federal Reserve Note injected into the banks is backed by overvalued collateral. When the U.S. was on the gold standard, the Federal Reserve Note was theoretically backed by gold collateral. The holder of a Federal Reserve Note could exchange it for gold. Today, the collateral backing the Federal Reserve Note is mostly federal government debt. If the price of this government debt is set by the market, it is reasonable to say the Federal Reserve Note can still be exchanged for gold at fair market value. With ultra-low interest rates and quantitative easing, however, the Federal Reserve has taken control of government debt prices and the collateral backing the Federal Reserve Note is now significantly overvalued.

Suppose interest rates returned to the 4% range which equals the expected nominal GDP growth rate in the future. The value of the collateral backing the Federal Reserve Notes would decline by around 14%. The overvaluation is a function of the sensitivity of the Federal Reserve's bond portfolio, referred to as portfolio duration, and the amount of interest rate repression or change in interest rates (Equation 5).

Equation 5: Overvaluation of Collateral

$$\textit{OverValuation of Collateral} = \textit{PortfDuration} * \textit{IntRateRepression}$$

In 2013, the U.S. dollar bill is backed by collateral only worth 86 cents if interest rates were to return to a more normal 4% (Figure 12).

The future inflation or currency devaluation as a percent of GDP that is building up can be measured using the ratio of Federal Reserve assets to GDP, around 20% in 2013, and the overvaluation of the Federal Reserve Note.

Equation 6: Inflation Buildup

$$\textit{Inflation Buildup} = \textit{Fed Assets} / \textit{GDP} * \textit{Overvaluation of Collateral}$$

Assume the following as representative of the U.S. in 2013,

- A Federal Reserve portfolio duration of 8.1 years
- Interest rate repression of 2.1% (i.e., an increase in interest rates from 1.9% to 4%)
- Federal Reserve Assets equal to 20% of GDP

Using these values, the implied buildup in inflation or devaluation in the 2013 U.S. dollar is approximately 3.4% of GDP.

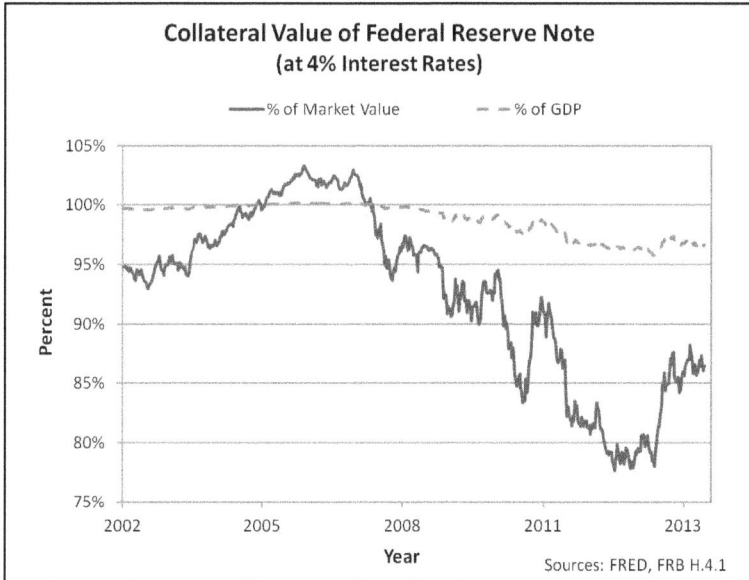

Figure 12: Collateral Value of Federal Reserve Note

Figure 12 provides an overview of the devaluation of the U.S. dollar as quantitative easing has progressed. The solid blue line shows that collateral value of the Federal Reserve Note if interest rates returned to 4%. The dashed red line shows the amount of inflation building up by taking its difference from 100%. A 10% inflationary buildup would correspond to the dashed red line at 90% in Figure 12. The longer quantitative easing continues, the larger the ratio of Federal Reserve assets to GDP may become and the more likely an inflationary confrontation may break out.

The tipping point is a product of the amount of assets the central bank owns and the amount of interest rate repression in the economy. Here, interest rate repression refers to the amount that interest rates are held below nominal GDP growth rates. <u>The more interest rate repression there is, the less a central bank has to own before reaching the tipping point.</u>

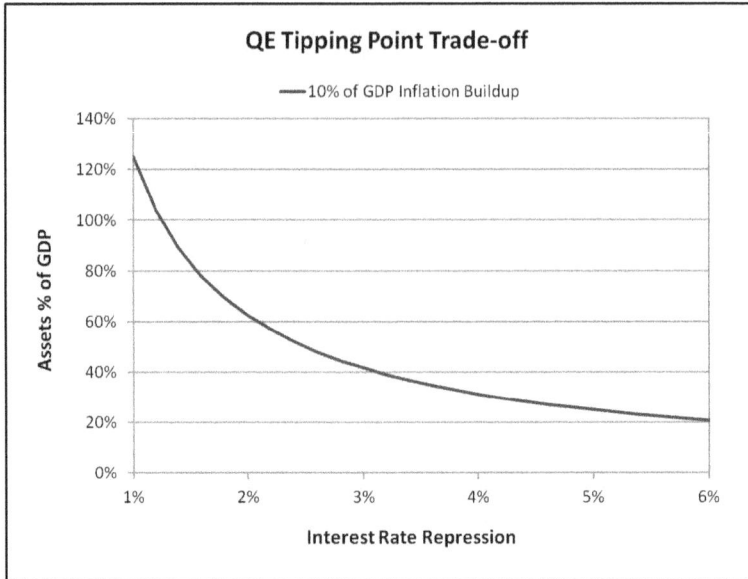

Figure 13: QE Tipping Point Trade-off

If the tipping point is equal to an inflation buildup of 10% of GDP, Figure 13 illustrates the level of Federal Reserve assets as a percent of GDP that would produce the tipping point for a given amount of interest rate repression.

With interest rate repression of approximately 2%, the Federal Reserve could increase its balance sheet to 60% of GDP before it would reach an inflationary buildup of approximately 10% of GDP. However, rising inflation could increase the amount of interest rate repression. Once the tipping point is reached, the Federal Reserve would have to find a way to restore confidence with higher interest rates and less central bank monetization.

Without structural reform or higher taxes, the Bank of Japan could reach the assumed tipping point of an inflationary buildup equal to 10% of GDP around 2017. If currency speculation takes over, the Bank of Japan could face the same situation as the German central bank during the 1920s; having to choose whether to accommodate capital flight or raise interest rates and possibly bankrupt the government. Most likely, they will impose capital controls on their citizens to avoid hyperinflation.

The second danger to quantitative easing is that it may pit the well-being of the federal government against the well-being of the banks in the future. Because the Federal Reserve pays interest on reserves, quantitative easing is a viable option to support the economy for a short while. However, the interest rate paid on reserves must be more than the cost of bank deposits (including the cost of deposit insurance). If future policy results in the interest rate paid on reserves being less than the cost of bank deposits, the reserves created by quantitative easing create bank losses and siphon capital from the banking system. The European Central Bank (ECB) has already instituted negative interest rates on bank reserves (ECB, Why has the ECB introduced a negative interest rate?, 2014). If the reserves are a small percentage of bank assets this is not a problem, however, with quantitative easing these reserves are becoming a larger share of bank assets. A highly indebted government may object to paying interest on reserves while the banking system largely relies on bank deposits for its funding which are subject to investor sentiment and capital flight.

Quantitative easing has saved the U.S. economy from an economic collapse but it is not an alternative to responsible policy making. If pursued on a large scale, eventually it will unleash inflation, currency devaluation, and capital flight. Over the last 20 years, the global economy has been a victim of creeping economic authoritarianism by the central banks. What started as low rates, then ultra-low rates, has now morphed into large-scale quantitative easing akin to monetary fois gras.

Understanding Inflation

Inflation is defined as the general rise in prices and is considered a monetary event in which too much money is chasing too few goods. This is misleading. This section will examine the different types of inflation, what causes them, and how inflation is related to money and credit growth.

Economists distinguish between three types of inflation, cost-push, demand-pull, and built-in inflation (Gordon, 2011). Cost-push inflation is when the price of products or services rise because the cost of production has risen. An example of cost-push inflation is when a supply shortage develops due to some external event and leads to higher prices. Demand-pull inflation is when the rising demand for goods leads to higher prices. For example, an increase in import prices would make domestic products more competitive and could increase prices due to the increase in demand for domestic products. Built-in inflation involves market participants trying to keep up with prices and is related to inflation expectations.

However, market power (Harvey, 2011) is the most important source of inflation and it is vital to understanding inflation. Market power is the ability to set prices due to a lack of competition. If one views the economy as an income pie, market power is the attempt to take a larger portion of the income pie for your constituents. Examples of market power include a company trying to raise prices, a union trying to raise wages, a commodity supplier trying to raise prices, an investor demanding a higher interest rate for a certain investment. All of these examples involve a group trying to take a larger portion of the economic pie from other participants in the economy. Recognizing how important market power is to inflation makes it easier to understand when inflation is a threat to an economy.

Milton Friedman is quoted as saying "Inflation is always and everywhere a monetary phenomenon." (Friedman M. , The Counter-Revolution in Monetary Theory, 1970). To understand this quote we will focus on the words "monetary phenomenon".

As participants in the economy with market power compete for their share of the income pie, debt growth may result to meet the demands of higher prices and market power. This debt growth can take the form of 1) money growth where the Federal Reserve or the banking system increases deposits in the economy, or 2) credit growth where foreign central banks' purchases of U.S. government debt or home equity extraction is used to meet the demands of higher prices. If one only looks at money growth, then the monetary phenomenon is weakened in the short-term. Including both money growth and the portion of credit growth that can be "printed" (e.g., home equity extraction) is a more accurate description of the monetary phenomenon. It is debt growth that is a companion to inflation as the real economy borrows to meet the demands of higher wages or prices or else total profits in the economy may fall.

Given that vendor financing is relatively stable and credit growth is limited by the size of the trade deficit or rising home values, to get large sustainable increases in inflation, eventually money growth is needed. When discussing money growth and inflation, "<u>accommodation</u>" is the most appropriate word.

As participants with market power compete for a larger share of the income pie, it eventually falls on the Federal Reserve to allow the higher wages or prices to take hold. If the Federal Reserve withholds money growth when credit growth is rising too fast, the general rise in prices will not be sustained. There may be changes in the relative price of goods, but the overall price trend will not rise above the Fed's target. This is why inflation expectations are so important. If all of the participants in the economy believe the Federal Reserve will accommodate higher inflation, then wage demands and commodity price hikes will become self-fulfilling.

Productivity gains mitigate inflation (Yellen, Productivity and Inflation, 2005). As productivity improves, the cost to produce a product or service falls and this lower cost can then result in lower selling prices. Productivity also affects profits available to the economy because the more productivity gains an economy achieves, the more debt growth can increase without inflationary consequences. In other words, productivity gains allow debt to be created from the money multiplier effect without inflation. If productivity is strong enough, it is possible that deflation can occur. However, while most deflation is damaging to an economy (Krugman, 2010), deflation due to large jumps in productivity is good and should not be countered with additional debt growth beyond the threshold of creating sustainable profits. Otherwise, this additional debt growth could induce a profit bubble and encourage foolish investments.

The reduction in U.S. inflation since the 1980's is partly due to the U.S. government controlling and hiding/deferring the market power of economic players. By allowing trade deficits financed by foreign central banks to rise, U.S. workers were put under greater pressure to compete with foreign workers. By giving public workers large pension benefits rather than wage increases and borrowing money from foreign central banks, government was able to hide and defer the market power costs of public unions. By confronting monopolistic business practices, government was able to lower prices for consumers (Klein, 2008). Strong productivity gains also played a role in lowering inflation.

The lack of inflation since the financial crisis, even with quantitative easing, is due to domestic workers having to compete with foreign workers while the demand for cash rises amongst the non-working population. The non-working population, retirees and students, do not have market power to induce wage inflation. Government spending on entitlements for the non-working population financed by quantitative easing does produce profits and additional bank deposits but these deposits have remained within the business and non-working household sector. In effect, quantitative easing has been meeting the rising demand for cash balances by the elderly and business rather than inducing business investment or higher wages. To generate inflation due to capital flight from the U.S. dollar, there has to be a better investment alternative than the U.S. To date, there is not. However, if income taxes are raised on the working population to pay for the benefits promised to the non-working population, demands for higher wages will ignite. The coming battle between tax hikes or benefit cuts will also be a battle between inflation and deflation.

Various groups with market power will at some point challenge the Fed by demanding higher prices and/or higher wages. It will be up to the Fed to accommodate them or confront them. The Federal Reserve will eventually have to transition its policy from "financial repression" of savers to "wage or price repression". However, they have demonstrated in the past and even in 2013 with a record profit bubble a reluctance to be criticized politically and instead have accommodated excessive debt growth (Boettke & Smith, 2012).

The larger the government debt/GDP ratio becomes, especially as it surpasses 100% of GDP and interest costs become a larger share, the more likely it is that the Federal Reserve will be confronted. If the U.S. federal government does not increase business investment through balanced trade and reduce its budget deficits, the Federal Reserve may find itself between a rock and a hard place, between confronting the U.S. government or accommodating higher inflation and inflation expectations.

While some pundits fear hyperinflation, large quantities of non-productive investments and financial repression are necessary to generate hyperinflation. Hyperinflation is both a monetary and a fiscal event (Fergusson, 2010). Non-productive investments are necessary because productive investments have the ability to repay investors without the assistance of monetary authorities. Financial repression is necessary to induce the capital flight that fuels the hyperinflation. If the central bank stops purchasing the non-productive debt or restricts bank lending, eventually the non-productive spending will cease.

During Germany's hyperinflation in the 1920s, interest rates were held about 8% below inflation levels and were accompanied by high tax rates. This financial repression along with the willingness to pay war reparations was the fuel that led to capital flight. Once capital flight began, it led the vicious circle of hyperinflation (Dalio, 20012). Capital flight led to monetization which led to further capital flight. The central bank monetization was an *accommodation* of currency speculation and capital flight. German stocks actually became cheap during the hyperinflationary period because it was better to have your money out of Germany than invested in tangible assets in Germany. The devaluation of the currency made Germany competitive but the financial repression and uncertainty made investment within Germany foolish. It was the household and business sector which confronted the government by boycotting investment in Germany. Only after the government economically destroyed Germany, did the government finally relent and end its financial repression through the introduction of a new currency.

Capital flight can be viewed as a form of economic democracy. When governments become too corrupt, the money leaves. Today, corrupt governments use capital controls to reduce the potential for hyperinflation. Capital controls are laws that prevent citizens from holding foreign currency or transacting in foreign exchange markets. Capital controls make it harder for the private sector to boycott investment in a country.

More likely than hyperinflation is a situation where 1) the market witnesses monetization to fund excessive budget deficits and 2) groups with market power try to defend their portion of the income pie with demands for wage or price increases and inflation starts to rise. The rising inflation increases financial repression and this causes all groups with market power to compete with greater and greater demands. Eventually, the political cycle swings towards stopping the monetization and balance is gradually restored to an economy.

Most people rightly consider inflation a form of financial repression. It confiscates wealth that is backed by financial savings rather than tangible property. However, taxing inflated gains is an even greater form of financial repression as will be discussed in Chapter 9.

Market power, debt growth, and central bank accommodation are the keys to understanding inflation. Modifying Milton Friedman's famous quote, inflation is always and everywhere a monetary *accommodation*.

Jackson and the Gold Standard

Andrew Jackson is one of the most interesting Presidents of the United States. He lacked a formal education and spelled like a 1st grader. His opponents, generally elites from the East Coast, questioned his lack of intelligence and pointed to his spelling as proof. In reply Jackson is quoted as saying, "It is a damn poor mind indeed which can't think of at least two ways to spell any word" (Wikiquote - Andrew Jackson, 2012).

Jackson was very religious and deeply cared about the laborer and Western pioneer. He witnessed speculative debt bubbles starting in 1817 when states like Kentucky set up government-run banks to provide credit to the new arrivals. After the debt bubble collapsed, there was a period of several years in which liquidation occurred and many pioneers lost the land that they had cleared and worked and lost their savings to the moneyed interest from the East Coast (Scallon, 2009). This experience and his economically conservative nature led him to call bank money "rag money". It is a historical irony that Andrew Jackson is on the $20 Federal Reserve Note made of cloth. He avoided debt when he could and paid off the entire U.S. government debt while he was President. He believed that the laborer needed a currency backed by gold or silver so that the laborer could not be taken advantage of by the moneyed interest (Remini, 1984).

In a political battle over the charter renewal for the Second Bank of the US, which he successfully opposed, Andrew Jackson is purportedly quoted as saying the following which resonates today given the results of the U.S. charter of Fannie Mae and Freddie Mac and their government guarantees of mortgages. History does repeat itself.

"Gentleman, I have had men watching you for a long time and I am convinced that you have used the funds of the bank to speculate in the breadstuffs of the country. When you won, you divided the profits amongst you, and when you lost, you charged it to the bank. You tell me that if I take the deposits from the bank and annul its charter, I shall ruin ten thousand families. That may be true, gentlemen, but that is your sin! Should I let you go on, you will ruin fifty thousand families, and that would be my sin!"(Henkels, 1928).

The gold standard is a means by which the value of the currency is backed by gold. If a bank depositor can demand gold instead of a paper note, then the banking system must have enough gold to meet the potential demands of depositors for gold. Advocates of the gold standard want all of the currency in a financial system backed by gold in a vault. Once an initial conversion rate is determined between gold and the new money, the money supply will depend on the amount of gold that the country acquires.

The problem with the gold standard is that if a country discovers a large quantity of gold, you get inflation because now there is more gold and thus more currency. If a country sells gold to another country for some product, usually during a war, a country may experience deflation as wages would be forced lower to reflect less currency as a result of less gold. The gold standard played an important role in the Great Depression. Advocates of the gold standard recognize this flaw but believe that this system provides long-term price stability, avoids financial repression, and is better than the alternatives.

Regardless of the advantages and disadvantages, the gold standard is still a political system and is only as good as the political courage of a country. Countries still found ways to cheat or appealed to patriotism until they were forced to admit that they didn't have the gold they were supposed to have or needed. A good monetary system requires political courage no matter what is backing the currency. No system will protect a country from inflation if it lacks political courage to confront the political forces when they want to bend the rules or take a larger piece of the income pie. Political courage requires an educated population to allow policymakers to take a stand against accommodation.

Sustainable After-Tax Profits

For the U.S. economy, a sustainable level of after-tax profits as a percent of GDP is around 5%. This is not simply because 5% is the average percentage in Figure 14.

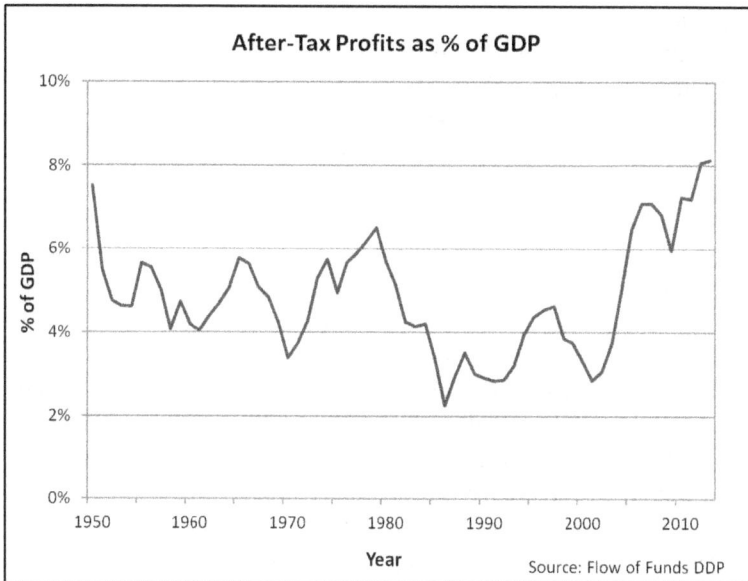

Figure 14: After-Tax Profits as % of GDP

After-tax profits equal to 5% of GDP is sustainable because it can be related to an inflation target, historical productivity, and dividend recycling assuming a stable level of debt to GDP. The sum of the Inflation Target and Productivity components should match the growth in three of the sources of financing profits, Vendor Financing, Bank Credit and Central Bank Monetization.

Equation 7: Sustainable After Tax Profits Example

Sustainable After-Tax Profits	*= Inflation Target (1.5%)*
	+ Productivity (2%)
	+ Dividend Recycling (1.5%)

Profits represent a return on capital. Since a company's return on capital depends on the inflation rate, it makes sense that a sustainable level of profits as a percent of GDP should also depend on the average long-term inflation rate. All else being equal in a steady state, the creation of money by the banking system generates inflation and produces profits when the debt proceeds are used to purchase goods and services included in the GDP.

Productivity also generates profits because it allows debt to be created without causing inflation. A country with higher productivity is able to create more money to keep prices stable. The creation of money by the banking system will produce profits when the debt proceeds are again used to purchase goods and services included in the GDP.

Dividend Recycling also generates profits. When a corporation pays a dividend to the household sector, the household sector is able to spend it and thus return it to the business sector in the form of profits. This is how a hypothetical economy that never changes (i.e. zero productivity and zero growth) is able to generate profits. Profits are earned by the business sector but all of the profits are returned to the household sector so that total market capitalization remains unchanged. The dividend income must be consumed to generate profits. If the dividend income is saved, profits will be reduced.

Equation 7 assumes a steady state in debt/GDP ratios and investment alternatives. Generating inflation requires viable investment alternatives. If wages are suppressed by trade imbalances and the creation of money is used to finance government entitlement spending for the non-working population, the link between profits and inflation weakens. Wage inflation may be delayed and replaced with higher cash balances until better investment alternatives are available.

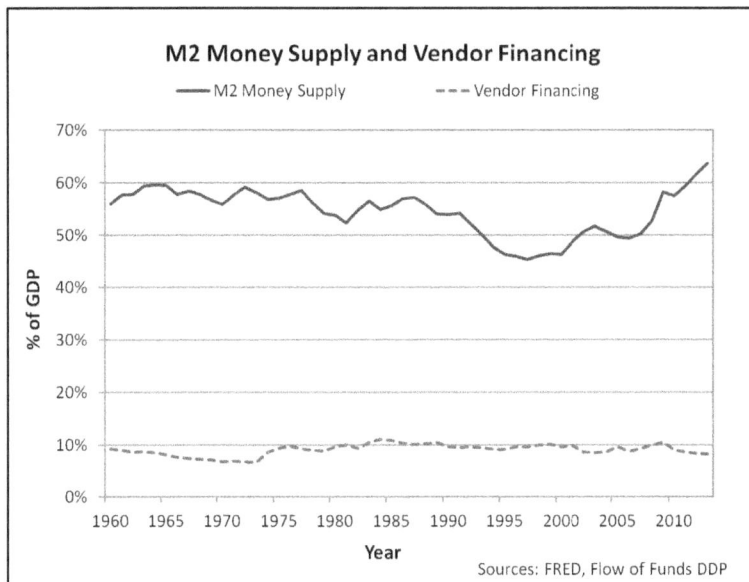

Sustainable after-tax profits can also be described in terms of the sources of financing profits. Figure 15 shows the size of M2 Money Supply and Vendor Financing as a percent of GDP since 1960.

Their sizes are pretty stable as a percent of GDP. The M2 Money Supply tends towards 60% of GDP while Vendor Financing tends towards 10% of GDP. Using the M2 Money Supply as a proxy to the combined size of the banking system and the shadow banking system's money market funds, the banking system's money multiplier effect should be able to finance profits equal to 3% of GDP if nominal GDP can grow 5% annually (60% of 5%). Vendor financing grows with the economy as well and should be able to finance profits equal to 0.5% of GDP (10% of 5%). Dividend Recycling may be able to generate profits equal to 1.5% of GDP and Central Bank Monetization can fill any residual balance.

If 5% of GDP is sustainable then why have profits as a percent of GDP risen to over 8% in 2013? The reason is that in the short-term there are two additional factors that can create profits but are not sustainable. The first is omitted inflation and the second is additional consumption due to quantitative easing.

During the housing bubble, inflation was measured using equivalent rent rather than home prices. By using income streams like rent rather than home prices, the inflation rate was underestimated.

Inflation was increasing and higher than the inflation target but was not being measured. Home equity extraction is a source of "credit supply" and like money supply can generate profits. It can create profits above what is sustainable but not for very long.

Additional consumption due to quantitative easing has been the primary fuel for record highs in corporate profitability in 2013. Because the central bank finances the government debt, the U.S. consumer is allowed to consume more. It is like pulling consumption forward. While it can generate profits above what is sustainable, consumption must return to the baseline when quantitative easing ends. If quantitative easing is continued indefinitely, it will eventually translate into higher inflation.

In this chapter we learned that credit supply created by foreign central banks and securitized mortgage debt is an important source of financing debt growth. It is not enough to just look at the money supply in trying to understand its relationship to GDP growth, debt growth, and profits. We also investigated why the Federal Reserve probably embarked on its quantitative easing programs. Without QE, the banking system or the U.S. saver would have had to invest almost 5% of GDP in the U.S. government to finance a portion of the budget deficit. We also discussed how important collateral is for debt growth and how the transition to a service economy may be causing a "collateral crisis" and making it more difficult to generate debt growth. We examined how market power and monetary accommodation are two keys to understanding inflation and how the gold standard requires political courage just like any other monetary system. Finally, we explored why after-tax profits equal to 5% of GDP is sustainable for an economy like the United States.

Chapter 5 – A Postwar History of U.S. Debt Growth

This chapter explores the rising Debt-to-GDP ratio of the U.S. from 1980-2012. Up to this point we have dealt with some economic preliminaries and discussed the frames that will be used to analyze the stability of economies. Now the analysis begins to understand what could have been done better and how to return to a more stable and prosperous economic system.

The Rising Debt/GDP Ratio

When measuring the debt burden of a country, economists use a ratio of Non-Financial Debt to GDP. Non-Financial Debt as its name implies does not include financial sector debt to avoid double counting. Therefore, it does not include the debt of banks, savings & loans, credit unions, broker/dealers, or insurance companies. It does include the debt outstanding for the household, non-financial business, and government sectors. The U.S. household sector's credit market debt outstanding is referenced from the St. Louis Fed's Federal Reserve Economic Data (FRED) database using the CMDEBT code. The U.S. domestic non-financial business sector's debt outstanding is referenced using the TBSDODNS code. The U.S. federal and state & local government's debt outstanding is referenced using the FGSDODNS and SLGSDODNS codes, respectively. Each data point is divided by its corresponding GDP to express the debt outstanding in terms of percent of GDP.

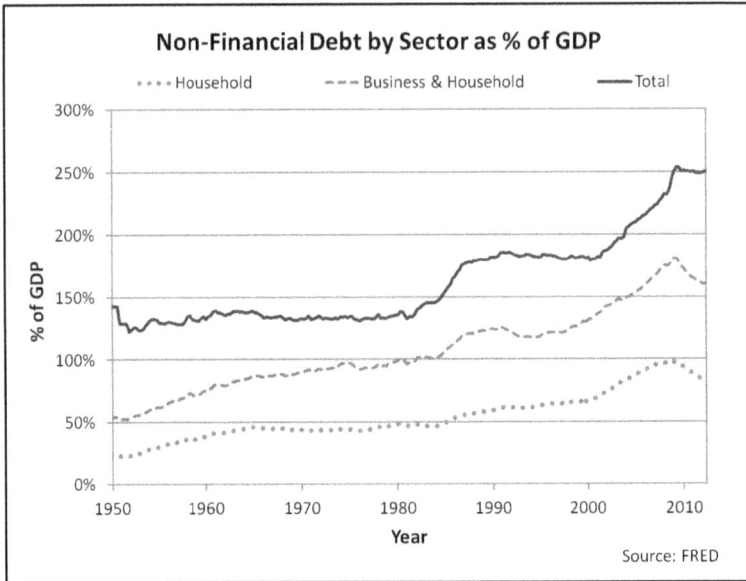

Figure 16 : U.S. Non-Financial Debt by Sector as Percent of GDP

Figure 16 stacks the household, business, and government sector's debt as a percent of GDP on top of each other. The increments or gaps between the lines identify the components of the total. It shows that the total U.S. debt burden of 130% of GDP was very stable until the 1980s. After 1980, the debt burden rises in stages and ends above 250% of GDP by 2012. During the post-war period (1950-1980), the government reduced its debt/GDP ratio while businesses and households increased their debt/GDP ratios. Then, starting from 1980, all sectors of the economy begin increasing their debt/GDP ratios. The household sector's housing bubble is visible from 2000. The government sector's large budget deficits are visible after 2008. The business sector has also been steadily increasing its ratio as corporations borrow in the U.S. to keep profits overseas and avoid corporate taxes.

The next step in our investigation involves looking at who financed the debt? Who lent the money? So far, we have only examined half of the information available to us because for every borrower there is a lender. To get a much better understanding of this debt growth, we can look at the other side of the balance sheet and investigate the lending sources of this debt growth.

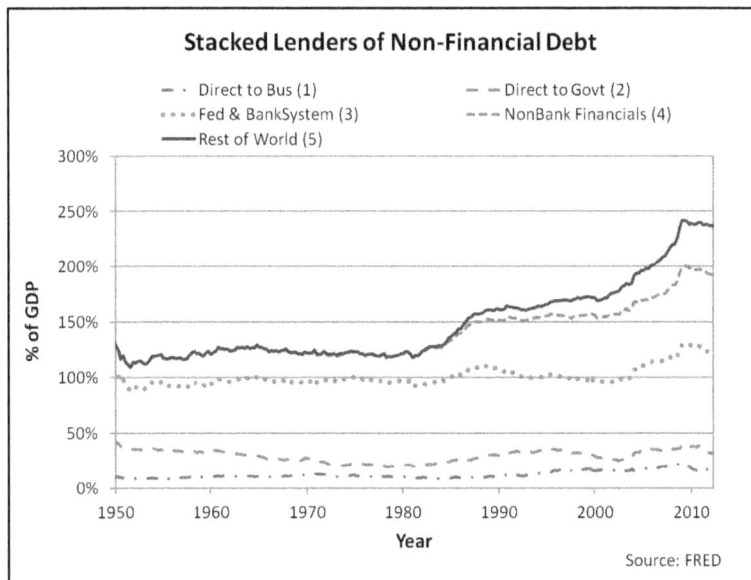

Figure 17 : Lenders of U.S. Non-Financial Debt as % of GDP

The sources of lending in Figure 17 are stacked and segmented to distinguish between entities who can create money and those who cannot. The Direct Savings components are lending from households directly to business or government (e.g., a household buys a Treasury bond or corporate bond in their brokerage account). The Federal Reserve and the Banks/S&Ls component is lending by the U.S. banking system. The Non-Bank Financial Institutions component is a form of non-bank lending such as from mutual funds, pension/retirement funds, or life insurance companies. The Rest of World component includes foreign central banks purchases of U.S. assets as well as private foreign credit investment in the U.S.

From Figure 17 it becomes clear that most of the growth in the Debt/GDP ratio from 1980 can be attributed to growth in the Non-Bank Financial Institutions and Rest of World components. The total of the Direct Savings and Federal Reserve/Bank/S&L components has been pretty stable at around 100% of GDP until a small increase from 2002. Since the U.S. has been running large trade deficits from 1980, it is not surprising to see that lending from foreign central banks and foreign private lenders now represents 45% of GDP. What is surprising is that the Non-Bank Financial Institutions component has increased significantly from 26% of GDP in 1980 to 72% of GDP in 2012.

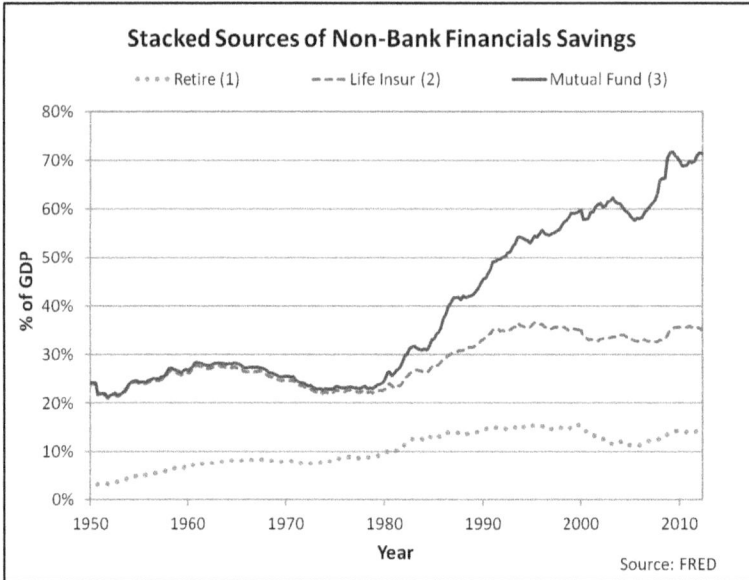

Figure 18 : Sources of Non-Bank Financial Institution Savings

Figure 18 illustrates that almost all of the increase in Financial Institution Savings as a percent of GDP came from the growth in mutual fund investments. The retirement savings component consisting of defined benefit pension plans, defined contribution plans, and IRAs also increased but not on the same order of magnitude as mutual fund savings. This leads to another question. Where did households acquire the money to invest in mutual funds? Did they reduce consumption and save or was there another source of money available outside of the banking system?

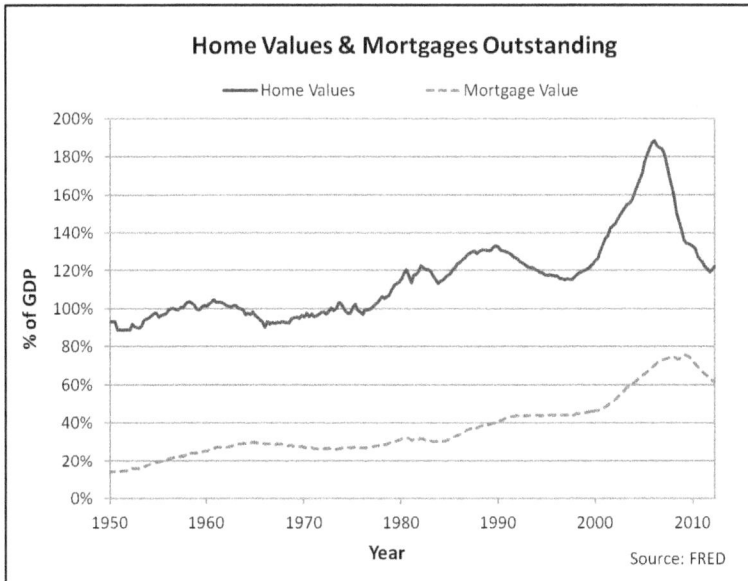

Home Values & Mortgages Outstanding

Figure 19 : U.S. Home Values & Household Mortgages Outstanding

Figure 19 provides the key to understanding where households obtained the money to fund their mutual fund savings. Mortgage debt has grown from around 25% of GDP in 1980 to as high as 75% during the housing bubble in 2008. Households have been taking money out of their homes and investing it in mutual funds since the 1970s. They shifted their savings away from tangible investments like real estate to financial assets instead. Without the growth in mortgage debt and extraction of home equity, the household sector would not have had the proceeds to invest in mutual funds. The final question in this puzzle is what happened in the 1970s to induce this shift in savings and how could it have happened outside of the banking system?

The answer is because the U.S. government decided to guarantee mortgages on a large scale starting in the 1970s. Fannie Mae and Freddie Mac were corporations chartered by Congress to guarantee mortgages and they were given an implicit government guarantee so they could borrow at low interest rates. Figure 20 illustrates the growth in government-backed Agency & Government Sponsored Enterprises (GSE) debt rising to 50% of GDP matching the increase in mortgage debt outstanding. Not only did the government guarantee the mortgages but it created mandates for Fannie Mae and Freddie Mac to buy up mortgages in the market and earn the spread between the interest rate on the mortgages and their government-guaranteed borrowing cost (History of the Government Sponsored Enterprises, 2012).

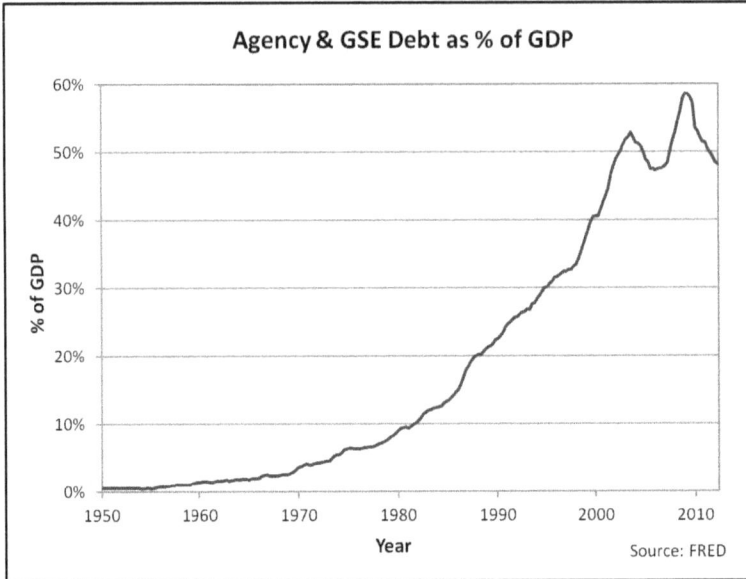

Figure 20 : U.S. Agency & GSE Debt as Percent of GDP

Since investors now had a guarantee and the government was bidding up home values through the mortgage purchases of Fannie Mae and Freddie Mac, households took advantage of the government policy and began extracting home equity and investing the proceeds in mutual funds. Households were able to obtain non-recourse financing and diversify their wealth in an environment of falling inflation.

The ability of the government to guarantee the debt without any additional government collateral was required for this to succeed. Trust in the government combined with the underlying housing collateral was all that was needed.

Returning to the original question of why the debt/GDP ratio rose from 130% to 250%, a summary of the evidence suggests that government debt had a willing buyer from foreign central banks and household debt was obtained from government guarantees on mortgages with the proceeds invested in mutual funds. While the increase from 130% to 250% of GDP looks like an overleveraged economy, it is mitigated by knowing that businesses have foreign assets and households invested their mortgage proceeds in mutual funds. If one nets the assets against the liabilities, the Debt/GDP ratio increases but not to the level of 250%.

If the U.S. government moves away from guaranteeing mortgages in the coming decades, it is possible that households would be forced to reduce their mortgage debt because of lower demand for higher risk mortgages and higher mortgage rates. If businesses are someday able to repatriate their foreign earnings without tax disincentives, businesses would reduce their leverage as well. Most importantly, if trade was balanced, the U.S. government would be able to reduce its budget deficits and through growth reduce its leverage.

Given our understanding of the growth in U.S. debt, what is a sustainable level of debt to GDP for the U.S. economy going forward? I would suggest that the government sector can sustain a debt/GDP ratio of 60%, the business sector can sustain a debt/GDP ratio of 60% after netting against foreign assets held overseas to avoid taxes, and the household sector can sustain a debt ratio of 60% as long as their mutual fund holdings equal 30% of GDP. When combined the total debt/GDP ratio would sum to around 180% of GDP before netting and 150% of GDP after netting mutual fund holdings.

When both the debt and the GDP are growing at the same rate, the ratio between outstanding debt and GDP doesn't change. Multiplying a debt/GDP ratio of 180% by the growth rate in nominal GDP we obtain the sustainable growth rate of debt. If the nominal GDP of an economy is targeted to grow at 5% annually, then the sustainable debt can also grow at 5% annually without changing the ratio. For a $17 Trillion U.S. economy in 2013, 5% growth is $850 Billion per year (5% of $17 Trillion) and the debt can grow by $1.53 Trillion per year (5% of $30.6 Trillion, $30.6 Trillion is 180% of $17 Trillion).

Flow of Funds Report

Every 3 months, the Federal Reserve releases the Flow of Funds report, also called the Z.1 report. It is currently available at http://www.federalreserve.gov/releases/Z1. In this report, the Fed tries to account for how much and what kind of debt is being created. There are hundreds of tables in the report. Some tables document the different entities that are borrowing or lending debt instruments. Some tables document what kinds of debt instruments are being created while other tables try to describe the financial situation of households or businesses. It is the most valuable economic report produced if one wants to understand the *financial* state of the U.S. economy and the actions that entities are taking. The data is two months old by the time the report is produced but economic situations usually change very slowly until a collapse occurs. From the report, one can construct how much debt the consumer, business, and government is creating and how profits are being created.

Table 8 provides a 33-year history of the U.S. source of after-tax profits as a percent of GDP and illustrates how the rise in the U.S. trade deficit during the 1980s lowered profits and led to the Plaza Accord to devalue the U.S. dollar. It illustrates how the Federal Reserve didn't do enough to support the economy during the S&L crisis in the early 1990s so the household sector had to save and finance the S&L bailout. It illustrates how the U.S. economy was close to balanced from 1994 to 1996. Then it shows the trade deficits beginning to grow again starting in 1998 with home equity extraction compensating for the trade deficit as Fannie Mae and Freddie Mac became more aggressive in their policies. We see the tech bubble around 2000 and the housing bubble peaking in 2006 with the household sector providing profits of over 9% of GDP. After the financial crisis of 2008, it shows the government sector massively supporting the economy with budget deficits reaching 10.67% of GDP. Finally, it shows record corporate profits as a percent of GDP in 2013 from the household and government sector financed by excessive quantitative easing.

The sector data in Table 8 comes from the following formulas and series names downloaded from the Flow of Funds report and expressed as a percent of GDP (FA086902005.A).

Sector	Household Sector	Non-Financial Business Sector	Government Sector	Trade Sector
Formula of Series Names :	+FA106060005.A +FA266060005.A -FA316231005.A -FA206231001.A -Next 3 Columns	+FA105019985.A -FA106300083.A	-FA315000905.A -FA205000905.A -FA224090005.A -FA344090005.A	+FA266903005.A

Table 8: Source of U.S. Profits as % of GDP (1980-2013)

Year	Household Sector	Business Sector	Government Sector	Trade Deficit	Total Profits
1980	1.18%	3.51%	1.44%	-0.46%	5.68%
1981	0.25%	4.19%	1.09%	-0.39%	5.14%
1982	-0.99%	2.30%	3.53%	-0.60%	4.25%
1983	-1.16%	2.52%	4.20%	-1.42%	4.14%
1984	-0.96%	4.55%	3.15%	-2.54%	4.19%
1985	-0.75%	3.40%	3.34%	-2.62%	3.37%
1986	-0.91%	2.52%	3.51%	-2.87%	2.25%
1987	0.92%	2.42%	2.57%	-2.97%	2.94%
1988	1.40%	2.30%	1.89%	-2.08%	3.51%
1989	0.46%	2.41%	1.66%	-1.53%	3.00%
1990	-0.70%	2.27%	2.64%	-1.30%	2.91%
1991	-1.66%	1.64%	3.32%	-0.46%	2.84%
1992	-2.63%	1.80%	4.22%	-0.53%	2.86%
1993	-1.56%	2.20%	3.51%	-0.95%	3.21%
1994	0.24%	2.80%	2.19%	-1.27%	3.96%
1995	0.58%	3.09%	1.86%	-1.17%	4.36%
1996	1.92%	3.05%	0.76%	-1.19%	4.53%
1997	2.57%	3.80%	-0.56%	-1.18%	4.62%
1998	3.70%	3.70%	-1.76%	-1.79%	3.85%
1999	4.75%	3.81%	-2.10%	-2.70%	3.75%
2000	5.94%	3.95%	-2.87%	-3.69%	3.33%
2001	4.80%	2.22%	-0.70%	-3.47%	2.84%
2002	2.97%	1.42%	2.55%	-3.87%	3.07%
2003	3.03%	1.39%	3.68%	-4.35%	3.74%
2004	4.95%	1.74%	3.31%	-5.01%	4.99%
2005	7.69%	2.14%	2.11%	-5.47%	6.47%
2006	9.04%	2.50%	1.05%	-5.50%	7.09%
2007	7.97%	2.36%	1.66%	-4.90%	7.09%
2008	4.90%	1.68%	5.10%	-4.85%	6.83%
2009	-1.37%	-0.62%	10.67%	-2.72%	5.96%
2010	-0.30%	1.00%	10.01%	-3.47%	7.24%
2011	0.86%	1.34%	8.65%	-3.66%	7.20%
2012	2.04%	1.98%	7.41%	-3.37%	8.07%
2013	4.58%	2.01%	4.50%	-2.96%	8.13%

Sector Profits	2005
GDP	**13,095,422**
Gross domestic product (GDP); sum of pieces FA086902005.A	13,095,422
Total Corporate Profits (6.47% of GDP)	**847,748**
Household Sector	**1,006,837**
Net Investment	864,299
Other	142,537
Trade Deficit	**(715,717)**
Non-Financial Business Sector (Net Investment)	**279,874**
Nonfinancial corporate business; gross fixed investment with equity REITs and inventories (IMA) FA105019985.A	1,189,794
Nonfinancial corporate business; consumption of fixed capital, structures, equipment, and intellectual property products, including equity REIT residential structures (NIPA basis) FA106300083.A	(909,920)
Government Sector	**276,754**
Federal government; net lending (+) or borrowing (-) (capital account) FA315000905.A	397,285
State and local governments; net lending (+) or borrowing (-) (capital account) FA205000905.A	159,718
State and local government employee retirement funds; total financial assets FA224090005.A	(182,437)
Federal government retirement funds; total financial assets FA344090005.A	(97,811)

Figure 21: 2005 Flow of Funds Source of Profits (FRB DDP)

In 2005, the Flow of Funds report (Federal Reserve Statistical Releases, 2005) reveals an economy with too much debt growth and the housing bubble in clear sight (Figure 21). The household sector alone was responsible for over $1 trillion in profits and total debt growth was responsible for over $1.4 trillion in profits in an attempt to overcome a $715 billion trade deficit. The total non-financial debt growth in the economy was $2.4 trillion in a $13 trillion economy where slightly less than $1.17 trillion was sustainable assuming a debt/GDP ratio of 180% and GDP growing 5% per year. It was only a matter of time before over $1 trillion in *household sector* debt growth and profits would be eliminated from the U.S. economy in a financial and economic crisis. This would become the trillion dollar cliff.

Without the housing bubble, the total U.S. profits in 2005 would have been close to zero. The $715 billion trade deficit would have offset the entire source of domestic profits. This is one of the reasons why the housing bubble was cheered on by markets and the U.S. government.

Sector Profits	2011
GDP	**15,533,845**
Gross domestic product (GDP); sum of pieces FA086902005.A	15,533,845
Total Corporate Profits (7.20% of GDP)	**1,118,297**
Household Sector	**134,262**
Net Investment	170,910
Other	(36,648)
Trade Deficit	**(568,739)**
Non-Financial Business Sector (Net Investment)	**208,592**
Nonfinancial corporate business; gross fixed investment with equity REITs and inventories (IMA) FA105019985.A	1,344,356
Nonfinancial corporate business; consumption of fixed capital, structures, equipment, and intellectual property products, including equity REIT residential structures (NIPA basis) FA106300083.A	(1,135,764)
Government Sector	**1,344,182**
Federal government; net lending (+) or borrowing (-) (capital account) FA315000905.A	1,400,082
State and local governments; net lending (+) or borrowing (-) (capital account) FA205000905.A	264,840
State and local government employee retirement funds; total financial assets FA224090005.A	(209,368)
Federal government retirement funds; total financial assets FA344090005.A	(111,372)

Figure 22 : 2011 Flow of Funds Source of Profits (FRB DDP)

In 2011, the Flow of Funds report (Federal Reserve Statistical Release, 2011) reveals an economy that is still generating too much debt and grossly out of balance (Figure 22). Government debt was responsible for all of the profits created in 2011 with its borrowings of $1.34 trillion larger than total profits of $1.1 trillion. The total non-financial debt growth in the economy was over $1.5 Trillion even though mortgage debt growth was negative due to foreclosures reducing mortgage balances.

The $1.5 trillion in debt growth was still in excess of $1.1 trillion in sustainable debt growth given a 2011 nominal GDP of $15.5 trillion with a growth rate of less than 4%. Once again total U.S. profits in 2011 would have been close to zero had the government sector ran a budget deficit of only $225 billion. Instead it ran a massive $1.34 trillion dollar deficit to not only offset the effects of the housing bubble but increase profits to 7.2% of GDP.

The Unfortunate Story

Over the last thirty years, the Flow of Funds data reveals a slow motion capital flight out of the U.S. where the business sector has avoided investing in the U.S economy unless there was some kind of bubble going on. Figure 23 illustrates the contribution that business investment has made to the creation of profits during the post-war period.

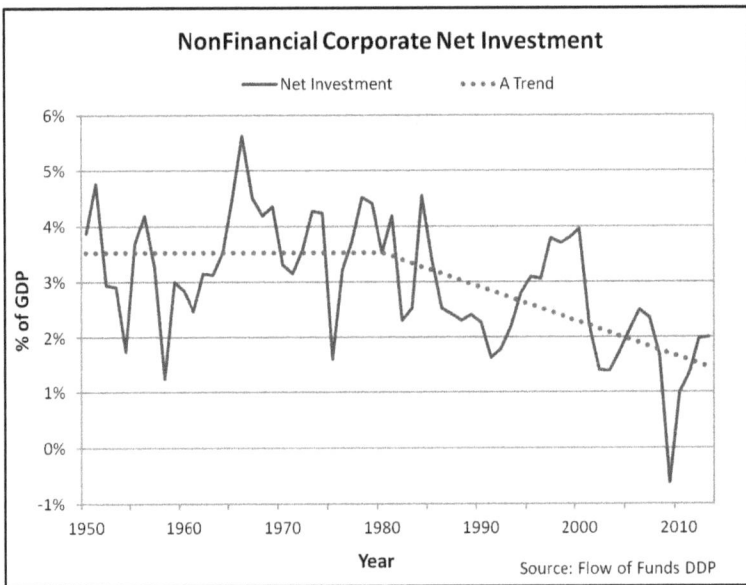

NonFinancial Corporate Net Investment

Figure 23: Net Business Investment as % of GDP

It clearly shows the roller-coaster economy that the U.S. has experienced since the mid 1990s. Net business fixed investment as a percent of GDP has been on a volatile decline since the early 1980s, from 3.5% of GDP to about 1.5% of GDP in recent years. Without the technology and housing bubbles, net business investment would probably have shown a steady decline from the early 1980's. Business investment would probably be below 1% in 2013 if not for the profit bubble due to excessive quantitative easing by the Fed.

While businesses have reduced their U.S. investments, the Federal Reserve has accommodated this slow motion capital flight with low interest rates, then ultra-low interest rates, and finally quantitative easing and monetization. To avoid a trade war or depression, government policy essentially incited a housing bubble until it blew up in 2007. Now, in 2013 they have orchestrated a profit bubble that relies on government debt and the support of the Federal Reserve's quantitative easing policy to generate profits of 8% of GDP when sustainable profits are most likely only 5% of GDP. Rather than address the issue of why businesses are not adequately investing in the U.S. they have tried to counteract the lack of business investment and loss of profits due to trade deficits with consumer and government debt growth. Unfortunately, business investment in the U.S. hasn't returned to its proper level and it will not unless significant changes in government policy are made.

Business net investment should be creating profits equal to around 3% of GDP on average and up to 4% of GDP when businesses and their banks are optimistic. When business net investment drops below 2% of GDP, an economy is sick and government policy needs to be reassessed to find the cure.

A Sustainable Balanced Economy

It is clear that the U.S. needs to transition to an economy that is stable and sustainable with all three sectors of the economy making *productive* investments in the U.S. economy and creating profits. Our sustainable economy will make the following assumptions,

- Sustainable After-tax Profits of 5% of GDP.
- Nominal GDP growth rate of 5% per year.
- Government Debt remains constant at 60% of GDP.
- Business Debt remains constant at 60% of GDP.
- Household Mortgage and Consumer Debt remains constant at 60% of GDP.
- The Banking System/Money Supply can finance profits equal to 3% of GDP.
- Vendor Financing can finance profits equal to 0.5% of GDP.
- Dividend Recycling can "finance" profits equal to 1.5% of GDP.

With these assumptions we can investigate the imbalances within the business, government, and household sector in the post-war period. In our sustainable economy, business debt can grow sustainably at 3% of GDP. This is just the result of multiplying the business sector's debt level of 60% by the nominal GDP growth rate of 5%. This 3% of GDP matches the business net investment that we desire for a healthy economy. Figure 24 again illustrates the U.S. Non-Financial Corporate sector's net investment as a percent of GDP and its deviations from a sustainable 3% of GDP. As just discussed, it reveals the weak business investment in the U.S. economy over the last 30 years unless a bubble of some kind existed.

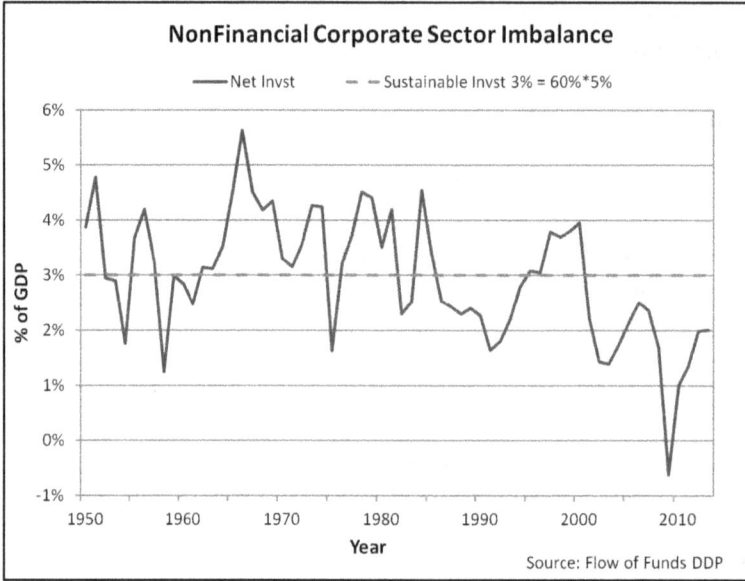

Figure 24: Non-Financial Corporate Sector Imbalances

In our sustainable economy, government debt can also grow at 3% of GDP. This is also just the result of multiplying the sustainable government debt level of 60% by the nominal GDP growth rate of 5%. Figure 25 illustrates the U.S. government sector's source of profits and its deviations from a sustainable 3% of GDP. It also shows the current projections of the Congressional Budget Office out to 2025. The U.S. government is currently projected to expand its budget deficits to almost 6% of GDP by 2025, double the 3% of GDP that is assumed sustainable.

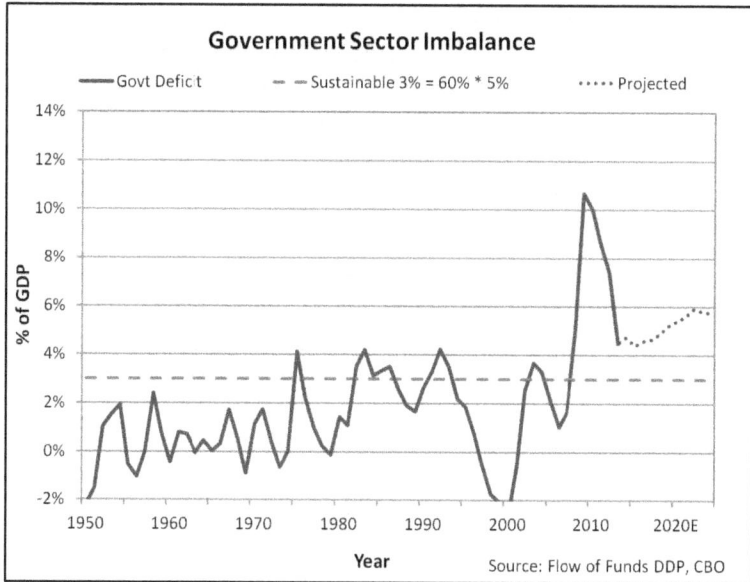

Figure 25: Government Sector Imbalances

Figure 26 illustrates the household sector's deviations from a sustainable economy. The sustainable household sector's source of profits equal to -1% is derived as follows.

1. For the business sector's net investment of 3% of GDP, we will assume this is financed by,
   a. Banking System/Money Supply: 2% of GDP
   b. Household Savings: 1% of GDP
2. The Mortgage and Consumer debt of 60% of GDP would create debt growth of 3% of GDP. We will assume this is financed by
   a. Vendor Financing: 0.5% of GDP
   b. Banking System/Money Supply: 1% of GDP
   c. Household Savings: 1.5% of GDP
3. The government sector's debt of 60% of GDP would generate a budget deficit of 3% of GDP. We will finance this with
   a. Household Savings: 3% of GDP
   Notice that in our sustainable economy the government budget deficit is financed solely by household savings.

4. Netting the household sector's debt and savings from the first three items above generates a household source of profits equal to -2.5%. The components are Mortgage and Consumer Debt (3%) and Household Savings (-5.5%). Adding Dividend Recycling (1.5%) as a source of profits from the household sector results in a sustainable source of profits equal to -1%.

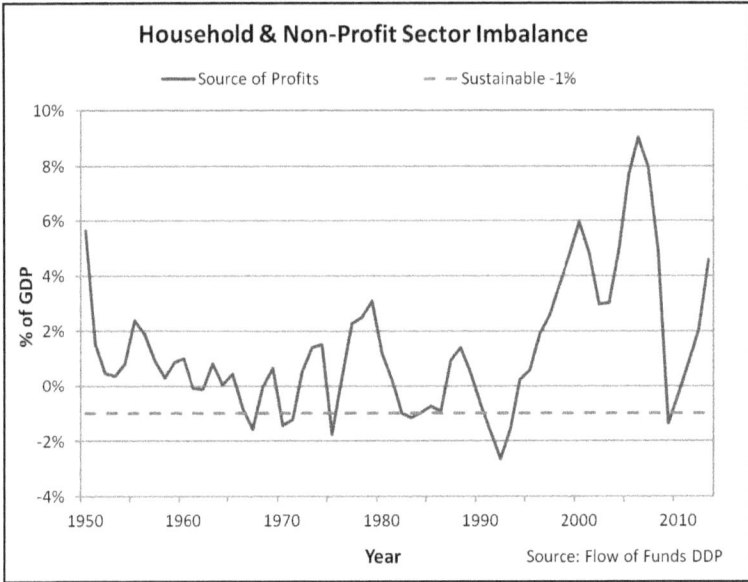

Figure 26: Household & Non-Profit Sector Imbalances

Figure 26 reveals that since the middle of the 1990s, the U.S. household sector has been called upon to generate profits at levels much higher than what is sustainable. Before 1980, the household sector's source of profits was also higher but the corresponding government budget deficit in Figure 25 was lower than what we have assumed is sustainable. Notice that in our derivation of sustainable levels, if the Government sector's sustainable budget deficit declined to 2% of GDP, then the Household & Non-Profit sector's sustainable source of profits could increase by an identical amount to 0% of GDP. This illustrates the trade-off between government spending and household spending if the banking system or quantitative easing does not finance the spending. The increase in the household sector's contribution to profits after the financial crisis of 2008 suggests that excessive quantitative easing has allowed additional consumption and record profits by financing government deficits so that the household sector hasn't had to and has induced a wealth effect from the appreciation of real estate and stock prices.

The three sustainable lines in Figures 24 to 26 add up to 5% of GDP as we initially assumed for profits. However, it is also worth clarifying that changes in our other initial assumptions would change this sustainable level of profits. For example, if nominal GDP grows at a rate lower than 5% then the Banking System/Money Supply and Vendor Financing sources need to reduce the amount of profits they can finance to maintain levels equal to 60% and 10% of GDP, respectfully as illustrated in Figure 15. The Dividend Recycling assumption of 1.5% may also be too large to be sustainable and a reduction to 1% would lower sustainable profits by 0.5%.

Given our knowledge of what a sustainable economy looks like, to restore balance to the U.S. economy, policies need to be put in place for businesses to want to invest an additional $200 to $400 billion in the U.S. rather than foreign countries. This additional investment would raise business net investment to its sustainable level of 3% of GDP. The $700 billion burden on household consumption, as represented by the household sector's imbalance of over 4% of GDP, needs to be eliminated by restoring balanced trade to the U.S. economy. Finally, government deficits need to be contained to no greater than 3% of GDP. This transition must also be a smooth and well managed, without spikes up or down, to avoid a depression or more bubbles along the way. The sooner it starts the better.

In this chapter we learned how the U.S. Non-Financial Debt/GDP ratio has increased from 130% to 250% as home-owners have larger mortgage balances due to government guarantees on mortgages but have invested the proceeds in mutual funds hopefully earning a rate of return higher than their mortgage rate. The debt/GDP ratio has also increased as the government tries to compensate for trade deficits, counter the effects of a housing implosion, and a decline in business investment over the last 25 years. We also discovered that the "credit supply", securitized mortgages and foreign central bank lending, played a much larger role in the debt increase over the last 25 years than the money supply. We looked at two snapshots of the Flow of Funds report to see a housing bubble in 2005 and an economy grossly out of balance in 2011.

It should now be clearer that the fundamental economic problems the U.S. faces are due to a failure to enforce balanced trade, a lack of business investment in the U.S., and poor economic policies over a long period of time. The U.S. is stumbling along reluctant to address the issue of how to restore balance to the U.S. economy. Government deficits with quantitative easing may keep the U.S. economy out of depression for awhile but if the government spending is targeted at consumption rather than infrastructure and other growth enablers, it will eventually lead to instability both politically and economically. There is no free lunch in economics, only justice.

Chapter 6 – The Importance of Trade Deficits

In this chapter we encounter one of the most important differences between the GDP frame and the Profit frame – the importance of trade deficits.

A trade deficit occurs when a country imports more goods or services than it exports to the rest of the world. In 2011, the U.S. imported $2.66 Trillion and exported $2.1 Trillion (13.8% of GDP) resulting in a trade deficit of $558 Billion (United States Census Bureau, 2011). In a GDP frame, the trade deficit looks small. For example, the U.S. $558 Billion trade deficit in 2011 was only 3.7% of a $15.5 Trillion economy. Why worry about this 3.7% of GDP? In 2011, the government budget deficit was much larger at $1.4 Trillion representing 9% of GDP (Federal Reserve Statistical Release, 2011).

Through the Profit Frame

Through the profit frame, the $558 Billion trade deficit of 2011 represented about 50%-60% of the almost $1 Trillion in sustainable profits for the U.S. economy. In a sustainable economy, business net investment should represent about half of the source of profits. When trade deficits come at the expense of business investment as illustrated in Figure 23, to the point of representing 50% of sustainable profits and reducing business investment growth in half from around 3.5% of GDP to 1.5% of GDP, its effects should not be ignored or discounted.

Could it be that other factors are resulting in weak business investment, like uncertainty, lack of skilled labor, business taxation, government regulation, lack of collateral, or an aging population? Possibly, but being able to compete and invest without taking enormous risk come first and second. Develop a list of industries that can't compete solely due to a lack of skilled labor or government regulations. Would it add up to $400 Billion per year? Would you invest in an economy when others are waiting for better opportunities to invest? Where the country is on the verge of a depression if the government doesn't borrow $1 Trillion per year? Where almost 100% of the source of profits comes from a government that is totally polarized and threatened with shutdowns? Where an economy needs a housing bubble to survive otherwise?

Trade is not just trade. There are multiplier effects. There is a need for stable debt growth and a balanced source of profits. When a business invests in an economy, it not only generates profits but creates conditions and incentives for other domestic businesses to invest. It is like a seed. Trade is good as long as each country stands up for its citizens and it is balanced.

This does not necessarily mean that certain industries like manufacturing must return to the U.S. It may be that other countries have a comparative advantage regarding manufacturing. Even if manufacturing returned to the U.S. it may continue to see a decline in employment due to automation. Whether it is manufacturing returning to the U.S., trade partners buying other U.S. products, or simply paying for U.S. intellectual property (these payments could replace government debt growth as a source of profits), a substantial share of profits should be created from U.S. businesses. When conditions are in place for business to invest in their community, everyone is nourished.

If an economy is unstable, the incentive to take risk, hire and train new employees, and start new businesses is diminished. When businesses are reluctant to invest, business profits decline, and the government or the consumer must compensate with additional debt growth in order to avoid a severe recession or depression. This is the story of the U.S. economy from the start of the 21st century. To avoid an economic decline, a housing bubble was cheered on with the federal government guaranteeing any outcome and abdicating supervision of its own guarantee to the "efficient market" that had multiple conflicts of interest from the home flippers, real estate brokers, appraisers, underwriters, rating agencies, and banks. After the housing bubble collapsed, the U.S. government stepped in with massive amounts of government debt growth to avoid a depression. Instead of addressing the problem of a lack of balanced trade and business investment, policies have been put in place to treat the symptoms. The result has been a declining middle class, rising income disparity, and divisive politics.

Currency Manipulation

Most text books that discuss trade are usually titled something like "International Trade and Finance". That is because trade and finance are like assets and liabilities on a balance sheet. This means that for the U.S. to run a trade deficit, some entity or individual outside the U.S. must finance it (Feenstra & Taylor, 2008). Financing is another word for lending.

Just like segmenting GDP and debt growth, one can segment the financing of the U.S. trade deficit. Some combination of foreign individuals, foreign corporations, and foreign governments finance a trade deficit. In the case of the U.S. trade deficit, it is being financed primarily by foreign governments and their central banks purchasing U.S. government guaranteed debt (Federal Reserve Statistical Release, 2011).

The following example is simplified to illustrate. If Toyota sells a car made in Japan to an American family, Toyota may receive $20,000. Toyota then needs to pay its Japanese workers and suppliers with the proceeds. If the foreign exchange rate, the rate that converts U.S. dollars to Japanese Yen, is 50 Yen per U.S. Dollar, Toyota would only get 1,000,000 Yen to pay its workers and suppliers. This might not be enough to earn a profit. What if the Japanese government or Japanese central bank gave Toyota 100 Yen per U.S. Dollar? Then, Toyota would get 2,000,000 Yen to pay its workers and suppliers. This might be more than enough to earn a hefty profit. When governments finance trade deficits, this is essentially what they are doing, and it is equivalent to a direct subsidy to an exporter.

Yet one question remains. Where did the Japanese government get the 2,000,000 Yen to buy the $20,000? When a foreign government buys U.S. Treasuries, they basically borrow money in their own local currency in order to pay for the U.S. Treasuries. Most countries have off-balance sheet government entities in which they borrow money in local currency and buy foreign assets. Even though a government is issuing local currency debt, converting local currency to U.S. dollars, and buying U.S. Treasuries, it will not show up as part of the foreign government's budget deficit because the value of the foreign asset will offset the government's local currency debt. Only the net difference in value will typically show up in the budget deficit over time as the exchange rate changes from the initial rate on the transaction date. This makes it easier to hide from the public the extent in which an economy is being propped up by its government borrowing money.

A foreign central bank can also buy U.S. assets to finance trade imbalances so that a government's off-balance sheet entity does not have to. Every year central banks determine how much money or bank reserves they want to create. Then, they must determine which assets to purchase to create the bank reserves. They can purchase domestic assets in their own local currency or they can purchase foreign assets. However, to be able to purchase foreign assets, they must exchange their local currency for foreign currency in the foreign exchange market. When this foreign exchange trade settles, the central bank simultaneously creates the local currency by creating a bank deposit and bank reserve. When a central bank purchases foreign assets, they are devaluing their currency and taking the foreign exchange risk necessary to finance trade imbalances.

If a central bank wants to buy more foreign assets than the quantity of bank reserves they want to create, they can sell domestic local currency debt in their inventory and replace it with foreign debt. When a central bank sells domestic local currency debt to buy foreign debt, this is called sterilization (Dominguez).

An alternative to sterilization as a means of reducing currency in circulation is raising the reserve requirements of domestic banks. The Chinese central bank has repeatedly raised the reserve requirements for its banks (Back, 2011). This is due to the large amount of foreign assets being purchased by the central bank and the subsequent money being created. So even though the Chinese central bank is creating Yuan reserves when it buys U.S. Treasuries, the Chinese banks are not allowed to use them but rather must keep them in their vault or at the central bank.

Now that we know how a government and its central bank finances trade deficits without causing inflation in their own country via sterilization or raising reserve requirements, we still do not understand why a government and its central bank would want to finance trade deficits and acquire foreign assets to the extent illustrated in Figure 3 in Chapter 1. There are several theories listed below that attempt to explain the incredible rise in official foreign reserves and we will examine them in turn.

- Countering Excessive Capital Flows
- Financial Stability Insurance
- Offsetting Short-Term External Debt
- Lack of Financial Market Development
- Follow the Profits

Countering Excessive Capital Flows

Economists recognize that large foreign inflows of money into a small economy can overwhelm a country. For example, excessive capital inflows can lead to a debt bubble if the addition of foreign lending produces unsustainable debt growth. All is well until the foreign inflows become outflows and the small economy is forced to reduce its leverage. Alternatively, excessive capital inflows can lead to an overvalued currency that destroys export industries of the small economy if the increase in demand for risk is not met with an increase in supply. During the European crisis in 2012, the Swiss central bank decided to cap the foreign exchange rate to the Euro to avoid the Swiss economy becoming so uncompetitive that lasting damage would be done to the real economy (Jolly, 2011). To protect the economy from this tsunami of money flowing in, the Swiss central bank purchased Euro denominated bonds to offset the capital flows coming in and sterilized their purchases by selling Swiss Franc bonds in their portfolio to avoid excessive debt growth. Faced with a similar problem, Brazil adopted an alternative policy of taxing foreign inflows to discourage excessive capital inflows (Reinhart & Smith, Too much of a good thing: The macroeconomic effects of taxing capital inflows).

While this explains why foreign central banks counter excessive capital inflows, it does not explain why they finance trade deficits. Some small portion of the growth in official foreign reserves may be a result of countering excessive capital flows, but almost all of the increase in official foreign reserves is due to financing trade deficits.

It is true that a central bank must guess what exchange rate should produce balanced trade, but they have guessed incorrectly for the last 35 years with the error always to their benefit and at the expense of countries like the U.S. forced to run trade deficits. It is not a coincidence. They have intentionally missed the target.

Financial Stability Insurance

As stated in Chapter 1, a typical guideline for the amount of foreign reserves to hold is equal to three months of imports. This is to provide liquidity and protection against a withdrawal of capital that could restrict the importation of necessary goods and services. In a crisis, a central bank can use its foreign reserves to cushion its economy from excessive foreign exchange swings and asset price volatility.

Yet the growth in foreign reserves has reached almost eight months of imports (Figure 4) and is much higher than the insurance required. The insurance theory explains some of the growth in official foreign reserves, to keep up with imports, but it does not explain most of the increase nor why these countries have consistently financed trade deficits.

Offsetting Short-Term External Debt

Another guideline for financial stability is to have at least as much foreign reserves as external debt (i.e., foreign-currency denominated debt) so that a country can pay off its foreign debt if necessary. It is referred to as the Guidotti-Greenspan rule. The foreign debt includes not only the government's foreign debt but the banking systems' foreign debts as well. Economists point to the Asian Crisis of 1997 as an example of the damage can be imposed on an economy when foreign lenders want their money back.

This theory claims that holding foreign reserves has a social cost to a country because the private debtors borrow at a certain rate while the central bank's foreign assets earn a lower rate. It suggests that this cost is willingly borne by a country to avoid the enormous cost that a financial crisis can impose (Rodrik, 2006). However, this situation is no different than any other bank. A bank must borrow at the deposit rate and invest in assets that earn a higher return. As we will discover soon, it is unlikely that there is any societal cost at all unless financial repression or bankruptcy losses are imposed on the central bank.

This theory also fails to explain the rise in official foreign reserves because the reserves have now reached multiples of the external debt (Rodrik, 2006). Like the other explanations, it explains why countries would counter capital inflows, in this case foreign lending, but it does not explain why governments and their central banks would finance trade deficits.

Lack of Financial Market Development

The final theory claims that these countries have underdeveloped financial markets (ECB, Financial Development in Emerging Economies - Stock-Taking and Policy Implications, 2009). As a result, a lender and borrower cannot connect directly through the bond market or indirectly through an intermediary like a bank so domestic demand is held back and firms face borrowing constraints. In terms of the profit equation it claims that consumers cannot borrow or lend and net investment is constrained. It also claims that due to asymmetric information and higher volatility, the private sector prefers to hold foreign assets.

However, this theory also doesn't hold water. First, it is not the private sector that prefers to buy foreign assets but the governments and their central banks. The central bank can finance profits if the money multiplier effect is limited due to a lack of financial market development without having to resort to buying foreign assets. Second, this theory is essentially implies that these economies are unable to generate adequate profits without running large trade surpluses. The profit equation clearly demonstrates that this is not true. Their lack of financial market development is due to their economic model in which the government crowds out private consumption and this has nothing to do with trade. Worker's Savings and Trade Deficits are not the same variable in the profit equation.

Follow the Profits

One of the reasons that so many countries have consistently devalued their currencies and built excessive official foreign reserves is because it is profitable not just for their business sector but for the governments. There is a flaw in the international system that makes currency manipulation profitable.

Governments do not tax other governments on their interest income and capital gains. So when a foreign government or central bank buys U.S. debt, it is tax-free (Fleischer, 2008). The higher the U.S. interest rates, the more tax-free income generated. Taking advantage of this tax-free income is one of the reasons global interest rates have been pulled towards zero.

This tax-free income creates a foreign exchange arbitrage that benefits currency manipulators. A foreign government collects tax revenue from its citizens on any future interest income when its central bank creates a bank deposit or sells a domestic government security to its private sector during sterilization. The citizens of the foreign country must pay tax on this interest income. This domestic tax revenue, along with the U.S. tax-free income, offsets the interest payments that the foreign government must pay to its private sector. This difference in tax treatment is like a foreign exchange tax arbitrage. Buy a tax-free asset (U.S. debt) and borrow at a tax-deductible rate.

Many have claimed that the financial crisis was due to the Federal Reserve holding interest rates too low for too long (CBS News, 2009). However, raising rates would not have induced business to invest in the

U.S. Had the Federal Reserve kept rates high to prevent a housing bubble, it would have only increased the amount of money that the U.S. would have paid foreign governments and their central banks to manipulate their currencies. Without the housing bubble, the U.S. economy would have needed large government budget deficits to generate adequate profits.

Each country should be allowed to decide on their own how they want to economically organize their country. History demonstrates, however, that most countries are not willing or able to pay the cost of income redistribution or excessive entitlements for long, so they must hide the cost. One of the best ways to hide the cost is to manipulate your currency under an economic doctrine called mercantilism (Vaggi & Groenewegen, 2003).

Studies have looked for evidence of mercantilism but have had difficulty finding any evidence (Aizenman & Lee, 2005). Perhaps it is because they are looking through the GDP frame instead of the profit frame. The evidence of mercantilism is not found in terms of increasing export market share but rather in terms of generating additional profits for their economy. The excessive growth in official foreign reserves has the same outcome as if these countries had set up a government-backed predatory bank to take business profits, add foreign exchange arbitrage profits, and invest in the steep yield curves of their prey to top it off.

When a government consistently undervalues its currency, it is also trying to control and pacify its citizens. By weakening its currency, a government creates a scenario where companies that produce and sell tradable goods look more profitable than they would be otherwise. This keeps employment high and possibly generates new jobs elsewhere as confidence is reinforced. It makes their citizens think that they are on the right track. Their system works.

Governments that manipulate their currency value political stability and order. The more business invests, the less the government has to invest to maintain stability. In most countries that manipulate their currency, the political calculation is that creating an export industry and transferring knowledge to their country is a safer path to development than trying to build a balanced economy with greater economic and political freedom.

It is much easier to hide currency manipulation from your citizens than it is to hide inflation. It is much easier to export the problem of creating jobs for an economy to another country by manipulating your currency. The decision to manipulate a currency is made at the highest political levels of a country by a handful of decision makers.

The Federal Reserve coined the euphemistic term "savings glut" for what is essentially currency manipulation (Bernanke, The Global Saving Glut and the U.S. Current Account Deficit, 2005). Yet, the foreign ownership of U.S. assets is concentrated in the hands of foreign central banks and sovereign wealth funds. Without foreign governments and their central banks buying U.S. debt, there would not have been a savings glut. The savings glut was not a phenomenon of billions of people choosing to save in order to lend money to the U.S., but rather orchestrated policy by a concentrated group of government officials and central bankers taking advantage of currency manipulation.

These central banks with large official foreign reserves could have devalued their currency by purchasing only domestic assets thus creating money in their banking system to be lent domestically. The Federal Reserve's quantitative easing program is an example of this policy. The Fed is not buying foreign assets to devalue the U.S. dollar but rather buying U.S. mortgage and government debt. However, the transmission from creating money to creating profits, a cheaper currency, and hopefully GDP growth is much more dangerous and therefore politically less reliable. For example, creating too much money to generate profits leads to speculative bubbles and excessive inflation once entities with market power challenge the central bank.

Currency manipulation through the mechanism described above is like exporting inflation although it may take time to show up in the country whose trade deficit is being financed. The "savings glut" was framed as "exporting deflation" because imports lowered the prices of goods (Kamin, Marazzi, & Schindler, 2004). However, if these foreign governments and central banks had not purchased U.S. debt, inflation in these foreign countries would probably have been much higher as the central bank would have had to print money to facilitate the creation of less productive jobs in their economies. These countries determined that buying U.S. debt and acquiring U.S. technology would be a more productive investment than any feasible government investment or safety net necessary to create jobs in their countries. It worked but it has put the U.S. in the position of requiring housing bubbles, large government budget deficits, and quantitative easing.

To achieve the level of profits that the global economy has today requires some central bank to adopt quantitative easing. By manipulating their currencies, these central banks forced the U.S. into low rates, ultra-low rates, and then quantitative easing. Had they not manipulated their currency, either profits would not be at record highs or the foreign central banks themselves would have been forced into quantitative easing to generate the equivalent amount of profits.

The Inflationary Accommodation of Oil

In the Middle East, oil is the main commodity and in some cases the proceeds are almost all profits. Clearly, the Middle East has a comparative advantage in oil production. The Middle East producers set production and limit supply to influence oil prices based on how much to profit from oil exports. Oil is their currency. If a typical central bank wants to buy dollars it prints money in its local currency. In the Middle East, they can "print" oil. Oil is a global currency accepted everywhere.

However, the price of oil is heavily influenced by the willingness of Western and Asian governments to borrow money in order to counter the loss of profits from trade deficits due to high oil prices. If governments did not compensate for high oil prices, one of the following three scenarios would be required to finance high oil prices:

Rising Oil Prices	Scenario 1	Scenario 2	Scenario 3
The U.S. Private Sector	Borrows	Sells Assets	Sells Tradable Goods
The Middle East Producers	Lend	Buy Assets	Buy Tradable Goods

Without the willingness or capacity of a country's private sector to borrow, sell assets, or increase exports, the amount of money allocated to purchasing foreign oil would be a constant and foreign oil demand would have to fall dollar-for-dollar with rising prices. Rising oil prices and thus a reduction in the number of barrels of foreign oil imported may induce a temporary recession but it would eventually lower oil prices and produce a sustainable equilibrium in the long-run.

If the governments of the developed world together demanded balanced trade with the Middle East and refrained from compensating for high oil prices with debt-financed economic stimulus, oil prices would be lower as the private sector would no longer be shielded by their governments' willingness to borrow and succumb to what is effectively currency manipulation by the oil cartel. This willingness by governments to borrow and fiscally stimulate their economy when oil prices generate trade deficits financed by Middle East central banks is a prelude to an inflationary accommodation. When the government debt is purchased by its own central bank, it becomes an "official" inflationary accommodation.

Failure Mechanisms

Eventually a country will have to stop its currency manipulation. There are several failure mechanisms. First, a government manipulating its currency must be able to borrow domestically in order to buy foreign assets. If the government doesn't have the money, it can't buy the foreign assets. Similarly, the central bank must be able to create money or sterilize the purchases. Since a central bank can usually create money, this is not a problem unless its citizens are politically opposed to additional inflation.

Another failure mechanism is if the country that is being manipulated (e.g., U.S.) stops borrowing money. This almost happened in 2008. When the housing bubble collapsed, it was only government borrowing that supported the U.S. economy and its trade deficit. Had the U.S. government not run trillion dollar budget deficits, there would have been minimal profits in the U.S. economy and the trade deficit would probably have collapsed along with GDP.

A third failure mechanism is when the cost of manipulating your currency outweighs the benefits, not in the long-term but in the short-term; because to a currency manipulator, any manipulation is better than no manipulation.

Some fear what would happen if the Chinese and other foreign central banks started selling their U.S. dollar reserves. Their fear is misplaced. The U.S. has its own central bank, the Federal Reserve. If China decided to sell its U.S. Treasuries suddenly, the Federal Reserve could buy them from the Chinese central bank. The Fed may decide it wants to buy them at a lower price but the price drop would be temporary. China would acquire U.S. cash by selling the U.S. Treasuries and be able to buy some other asset in the world, such as converting it back to their currency and buying domestic debt. The Federal Reserve would acquire the U.S. Treasuries which would increase the amount of bank reserves in the U.S. banking system. To avoid this new money from creating debt growth, the Fed could raise the reserve requirement and require U.S. banks to hold this cash in their vault or at the Federal Reserve, much like China has done. Moving the U.S. debt from one government central bank to another government central bank would just change the amount of money or money supply in each of their financial systems. To avoid excessive debt growth, each central bank could change their reserve requirements in their banking system.

The benefits of currency manipulation are visible in the profit frame. The official foreign reserves are like assets at any bank but they get tax benefits which leads to a foreign exchange arbitrage. In addition, the private sector gets additional profits to build upon domestically and pacify citizens politically. These additional profits can be directed anywhere in the economy, not just to expand export market share. If the U.S. wants business to adequately invest in the economy, the fundamental problem of currency manipulation must be addressed without punishing trade.

The Importance of Collateral

Another reason why trade is important to an economy is that tradable goods either are or depend on assets which can be used as collateral. Tradable products require inventory, equipment, and factories; all of which can serve as collateral for a growing economy.

Banks typically require collateral to make loans. If a business wants to invest but lacks collateral, it must resort to unsecured or equity financing which is more costly and difficult to arrange. When an economy outsources industries that banks lend to, it makes it harder to generate business debt growth in the economy as well as healthy, productive growth.

A service economy can grow side by side with a tradable economy, each assisting the other's growth. When too much of the growth burden is put on the service economy, then banks must rely more on business cash flows than collateral.

The Long-Term Consequences

The long-term consequences of the U.S. trade deficit can be seen in the decline of the middle class. The U.S. government has adopted a barbell strategy; support the poor and the rich but let the politically unconnected middle class fend for themselves. Without a government policy that demands balanced trade, the middle class have lost jobs to outsourcing and been forced to compete beyond the Ricardian theory of trade.

The Ricardian theory of trade or comparative advantage (Samuelson & Nordhaus, 2005) demonstrates that one country can have higher wages than another country in *every* industry and it will still be beneficial for both countries to trade. The reason is that each country will have different *relative* wages between industries. The country that has lower costs in industry A relative to industry B should export the products from industry A and import the products from industry B.

However, the Ricardian theory of trade assumes balanced trade. It assumes that governments do not finance trade deficits to make their industries look more profitable. When trade is not balanced, workers are forced to compete on absolute wage terms with foreign workers instead of relative wage terms under Ricardian theory. Each segment of labor negotiates its worth under game theory. Trade can change the balance of power, the value of rewards and threats, and ultimately the wage outcomes. The failure to enforce balanced trade partially explains why median wage gains in the U.S. have stalled for the last decade.

Some may blame corporations for this policy. A multinational corporation with a global reach may have many factors to determine where to place its factory. However, a businessperson is typically constrained from looking at the way the world *should* work to looking at the way the world *does* work. They see countries that can generate a profit for their shareholders, which have an advantage because the government is supporting a weak currency, and they invest in those countries. If they chose not to invest, they would be replaced by someone who would, either internally or through lost market share when competing.

Business may influence government policy, advocating short-term benefits rather than long-term needs, but it is the failure of government policy to enforce balanced trade that is responsible for the stagnation of the middle class. It may be true that "now is not the time in a recession to enter a trade war" (Huntsman, 2011), however, a solution exists to enforce balanced trade without punishing trade which will be discussed in the next chapter. If government policy enforced balanced trade and businesses were to invest in the U.S. again, the middle class would rebound.

If the U.S. continues to run large trade deficits, it risks having to rely on government budget deficits on the order of 5% of GDP to avoid an economic collapse. If an economy grows 4% per year and their government deficits as a percent of GDP are 5% per year, then the government debt-to-GDP ratio will eventually rise to 125% of GDP. Debt levels in this area tend to slow growth and increase the risk of investing (Reinhart & Rogoff, This Time is Different, 2011). Debt levels in this area also require interest rates to remain very low which increases the risk of inflation and capital flight.

If the government debt is spent on productive investments, this 5% of GDP can be viewed as a substitute for business investment. However, increases in entitlement spending to appease the middle class in the short term doesn't compensate for a lack of business investment. It doesn't cure the problem but just treats the symptoms until there is an inflation confrontation that further polarizes the middle class.

The U.S. government policy is two-faced. It declares it cares about the middle class, promoting entitlements and low taxes, while at the same time allowing foreign central banks to manipulate their currency at the expense of the U.S. middle class. The middle class doesn't see the government is taking from one hand to give from the other. If the U.S. did not have a trade deficit, financing the government budget deficit would become more transparent. Restoring a balanced source of profits could be politically difficult but on the bright side it would restore business investment, protect middle class households, and avoid a chaotic government debt crisis.

If or when the U.S. trade deficit shrinks, it will be harder for countries to hide their structural problems. They may have to resort to government spending and budget deficits or increased inflation if they do not want to make structural adjustments like reducing the size of government, improving labor mobility, and insuring competition. The global economy has not yet reached the end of the crisis that started in 2008. The first stage exposed the cost of poor government choices. The second stage will involve either paying for these poor government choices or changing their ways.

In this chapter we examined how a 3% of GDP trade deficit can represent 60% of the profits created in an economy. Over the last 35 years, foreign governments and their central banks have manipulated their currencies to finance the U.S. trade deficit, make their economies look more profitable, and generate political stability in their countries. However, this has come at the expense of the U.S. middle class who have had to compete to a greater extent on absolute wages rather than relative wages and are now burdened with financial repression and large government debts outstanding. The U.S. government would be wise to adopt a transparent, multi-lateral policy that represents its citizens without punishing trade. The next chapter will give us insights on how that may be achieved.

Chapter 7 – A Sustainable Global Economy

There is a policy that the U.S. can follow that enforces balanced trade without punishing trade. It is a policy that would be foolish to retaliate against without significant cooperation. It is a policy that the global economy could embrace and that would lead to sustainable growth. It is a policy based on science that utilizes cooperation and game theory. It is a policy that isn't arbitrary and doesn't discriminate against one country in favor of another. It is a policy that doesn't have to rewrite free trade agreements. It is a policy that doesn't pit one industry against another industry. Most important, it is a policy that doesn't punish trade.

The global economy needs a *sustainable* global solution in which deviations from balanced trade will return the participants back to balanced trade. If a marble is placed in the center of a bowl, it wants to remain there by the force of gravity. If the marble is nudged from the bottom of the bowl, the force of gravity returns the marble to the bottom of the bowl. The global economy needs a force like gravity that will return imbalances in trade back into balance.

The current global economic model has a flaw that has not been dealt with. Trade imbalances are profitable to currency manipulators. The incentive is not to return to balance but to take as much profit as possible from other countries. Governments can buy tax-free foreign assets while borrowing at tax-deductible interest rates and to top it all off generate additional profits for their economy. Hoping that trading partners will cooperate has not worked. Hope is not a strategy. To restore balance, the global economy must utilize game theory and adopt new rules.

Game Theory and Nash Equilibriums

If you enjoyed the movie "A Beautiful Mind" with Russell Crowe then you already know something about game theory (Myerson, 1991). The movie was about John Nash who won a Nobel Prize for his contributions to game theory and economics.

Game theory is a mathematical model of negotiations in which each participant has a set of potential gains they can achieve in certain situations and a set of threats that they can use in other situations. Each participant can join coalitions with other participants to increase their gains or strengthen their threats. Game theory then looks for solutions in which no player would be better off changing the solution if they acted alone. The key point is "if they acted alone". Each of these solutions is called a "Nash Equilibrium".

There can be many Nash Equilibriums. There will be an optimal solution but there is no guarantee it will be chosen in a negotiation. It will depend on whether the participants are able to find it while negotiating. To move from one Nash Equilibrium to another requires cooperation. There is also no guarantee that the solution arrived at is sustainable. It may be a solution temporarily until the parameters of the equations change, a crisis erupts, and then all the participants negotiate again for a new Nash Equilibrium.

This is the situation that the global economy finds itself in. The current global imbalances are not sustainable with the U.S. supporting itself with large government budget deficits and official foreign reserves increasing each year. The global economy needs cooperation or new rules to move to a new Nash equilibrium that is sustainable with balanced trade as theorized by David Ricardo.

Taxing the Portion of Official Foreign Reserves that Finance Trade Imbalances

Official foreign reserves are the foreign assets that governments or their central banks own. One solution to restore balanced trade is to tax the portion of official foreign reserves that finance trade imbalances. Not all official foreign reserves, just the reserves that finance trade imbalances each year.

When a government or its central bank is purchasing another country's assets, their motivation should be viewed with great skepticism. A government financing another country's trade deficit is neither free nor fair trade. It does not fulfill the assumptions of trade theory. It is predatory. If a country wants to devalue their currency, their central bank should buy their own local currency debt, create money, and accept the risks of bubbles, bad investments, and potential inflation. If a country is unwilling to print money in their local currency to restore balanced trade, they should then have to pay a tax on the buildup in their official foreign reserves that outweighs the benefits of currency manipulation and incentivizes governments to play fair and return to balanced trade.

The U.S. could easily assemble the information and reporting systems to determine the increase in official foreign reserves in U.S. dollars that financed the U.S. trade deficit. This system would be similar to those used to identify tax evasion, money laundering, and reports of the amounts due foreign entities in the Fed's H.8 Assets and Liabilities of Commercial Banks in the United States weekly release.

It would not make sense to change the rules of the game for past behavior and start a retaliatory economic war. Therefore, the current balances of official foreign reserves should not be taxed. The past is the past. Policy was flawed and one can say that justice was delivered. But going forward, government policy needs to change and the portion of additional official foreign reserves that finance trade deficits should be subject to new rules. These rules would provide an enforcement mechanism for balanced trade.

Perhaps a tax only on the income generated from the portion of official foreign reserves that finance trade deficits is sufficient to promote cooperation. More likely, a tax would need to be applied each year on the additional amount of official foreign reserves that finance trade imbalances. This would act like a wealth tax or a tax on capital. This tax rate would not have to be a large percent of the additional foreign exchange reserves in order to generate the required incentives. The tax could be structured to replicate the depreciation of an imported product. If a foreign government chose to purchase a financial asset rather than a product, the tax could act like an equivalent depreciation.

There may be cases where a small country is overwhelmed by foreign private investors wanting to invest in their country. In this case, it is reasonable to expect a country to increase its official foreign reserves to offset the private capital inflows without being subject to the tax. This policy would not tax them. However, a government building official foreign reserves should be held accountable for what exchange rate they use to counter the private capital inflows and whether it fosters balanced trade.

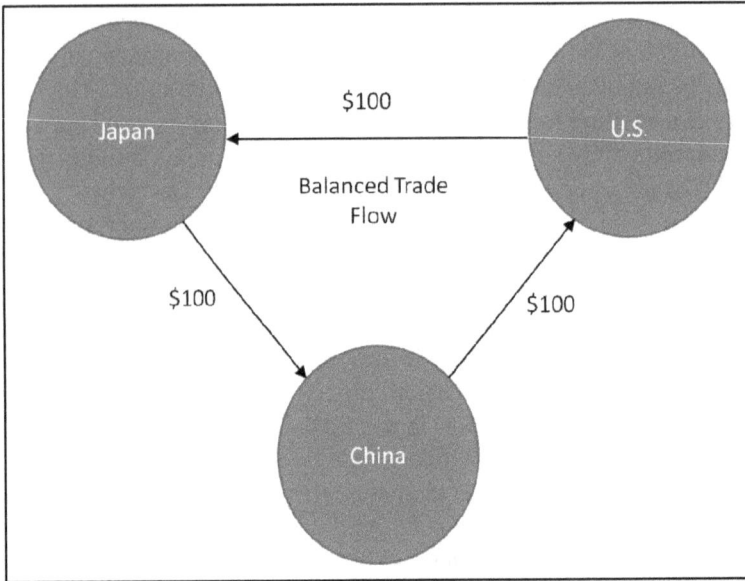

Figure 27: Example of Balanced Trade with Country Deficits

This policy also doesn't declare that every country in the world must have balanced trade with the U.S. As illustrated in Figure 27, each country can have trade deficits and surpluses with each other. For example, if Japan has 1) a trade surplus with the U.S. and 2) a trade deficit with China such that the surplus and deficit offset equally, Japan can exchange the U.S. dollars it receives from its trade surplus with the U.S. to fund its trade deficit with China. In Figure 27, the arrows point to the country with a trade surplus between the two corresponding countries. With balanced trade, the $100 just circulates and each country has balanced trade overall because what comes in to the country from country X goes out to country Y. In this situation, a tax would not be due because the overall trade balance for each country would be zero.

This suggested tax policy doesn't declare that the U.S. cannot run a trade deficit. A tax would not be imposed if the U.S. ran a trade deficit as long as the trade deficit is financed by the private sector; by foreign individuals and corporations choosing to invest in U.S. assets and taking the credit and foreign exchange risk that comes with it.

On the other hand, if a government or its central bank finances the trade deficit with a buildup in official foreign reserves, then the government or its central bank could be taxed by the countries incurring a trade deficit in order to incentivize a return to balanced trade.

In a multi-lateral world, each country with a trade deficit could assess an annual tax at a common point in time based on the year-over-year increase in official foreign reserves (OFR) held in its currency. Only a fraction of the OFR increase would be subject to the tax when a country's overall trade deficit was smaller than the OFR increase. The penalty for each country's additional official foreign reserves held in this currency could be attributed as follows.

Equations 8-12: Penalizing Official Foreign Reserves that Finance Trade Deficits

$Overall\ Trade\ Deficit = \Sigma_{Countries}\ Bilateral\ Trade\ Balances$

$Overall\ \Delta\ OFR\ in\ Ccy = \Sigma_{Countries}\ \Delta\ OFR\ in\ Ccy_{country}$

$Size = Min(-Overall\ Trade\ Deficit,\ Overall\ \Delta\ OFR\ in\ Ccy)$

$Fraction = Max(Size,\ 0\%)\ /\ (Overall\ \Delta\ OFR\ in\ Ccy)$

$Penalty_{country} = Fraction\ *\ TaxRate\ *\ Max(\Delta\ OFR\ in\ Ccy_{country},\ 0)$

The equations in the block above provide a simplified example of how a country with an overall trade deficit could attribute the tax or penalty to each country that increased its official foreign reserves in this currency. The appropriate tax rate could be a function of size and would need to be large enough to overcome the foreign exchange arbitrage and be a legitimate deterrent to currency manipulation.

If a country adopted this framework and did not have a trade deficit, the size of the penalty it would attribute to other countries would be zero. If a country did not have an increase in official foreign reserves held in their currency, the size of the penalty it would attribute to other countries would be zero. If a penalty was to be attributed, only the countries that increased their official foreign reserves in this currency would be subject to the assessed tax. It would make governments and their central banks think twice about what exchange rate to use to counter private investment flows when they are manipulating their currency.

It would also enforce cooperation amongst governments because each central bank would not want to be taken advantage of by another central bank. For example, given a U.S. trade deficit that would need to be financed, the European Central Bank (ECB) would not want to pay a tax to the U.S. because the Chinese central bank exchanged their U.S.

dollars into Euros and the ECB acquired them through sterilization. If the ECB wanted to counter this action, they would have to exchange these U.S. dollars for preferably Chinese Yuan in the foreign exchange market rather than hold U.S. dollar assets and pay the U.S. tax. The ECB would suddenly have an interest in determining which currency to hold its official foreign reserves. The U.S. would no longer be the victim of currency manipulation. The U.S. dollars obtained by currency manipulation would become a hot potato.

This tax policy doesn't target any country by name. At the beginning of the year, it would not be known who would be required to pay the tax or if any tax would even need to be paid. If everyone cooperates, there would not be a tax assessed because the private sector would finance any net imbalances. Governments and their central banks would get out of the business of financing large trade deficits and instigating quantitative easing wars.

The policy doesn't require the repeal of free trade agreements or any trade agreements at all. Trade and finance are like assets and liabilities. The trade agreements are dealing with the asset side of the situation. Taxing increases in official foreign reserves deals with the liability side of the situation and says nothing about what is traded. Together they allow countries to set their trade agendas in a framework that enforces fair trade and doesn't turn one country into a predator and the other into prey.

Another feature of the policy is that it automatically punishes retaliation. A country who adopts this policy doesn't have to make trade threats to achieve balanced trade. For example, if a country decided to punish the U.S. by reducing imports from the U.S., it would only increase their official foreign reserves and subject them to a larger tax on the now larger imbalance unless they found someone in the private sector willing to finance the increase in the U.S. trade deficit. Since the private sector is relatively limited in its capacity to finance large trade imbalances, any retaliation would most likely fail.

If a country wanted to run a trade surplus, this would not be taxed as long as the individuals and businesses of that country financed their country's trade surplus and took the foreign exchange and credit risk associated with it. The tax would be due only if their government or central bank financed their trade surplus, thereby acting like an insurance company that offered to guarantee its citizens and businesses against foreign exchange and credit losses.

It would make sense to have a de minimis threshold before the tax is due as a function of trade volume. This threshold should be set at a level so that the cumulative effect could not damage business investment in the deficit country to the extent it currently does.

This policy of taxing the portion of official foreign reserves that finance trade deficits is similar to how the flow of gold helped to restore trade balances when the developed world was on the gold standard. Since the global economy has left the gold standard in favor of fiat currencies and floating exchange rates, it has been struggling to find a policy that can restore cooperation yet allow changes in the value of currencies.

One area of conflict could be in deciding when investment flows are overwhelming a country and allowing a government to intervene. If a country imposed a temporary tax on private inflows like Brazil has done in the recent past (Girotto & Velloza, 2012), this could mitigate the flow of money to a small country. However, only a country with a trade deficit due to a strong currency would have a legitimate claim to intervene and buy another country's debt. Intervening to protect an overall trade surplus would subject them to the official foreign reserve tax.

A look-back provision is another possible provision that could help alleviate any differences of opinion. If a government intervened to protect its country from overwhelming investment flows, then a tax could be assessed later over a multi-year period. If a country intervened but ended the year with balanced trade or a trade deficit, no tax would be assessed. However, a country generating or protecting a trade surplus would be subject to the tax reflecting the size of the overall trade surplus. Governments, like China, who consistently make "bad guesses" about what exchange rate to use to counter investment flows, would be held accountable for their bad guesses.

This policy proposal is not without the potential for loopholes and circumvention. One of the most obvious forms of circumvention is to set up a company financed or guaranteed by the government that buys foreign assets. By claiming the company is not a government institution but rather a member of the private sector, there could be disagreements about whether a tax is due. The banking system of a country is the most likely to lend to another country with the implicit backing of the government. While there could be a disagreement, this alone would not prevent a government suffering from trade deficits from assessing the tax. A country could look at a bank's foreign assets and its foreign exchange risk and compare it to the bank's capital to determine if the ratio is excessive and the government guarantee of foreign exchange or credit losses is implicit. Along the same line, if a government bailed out bank depositors or creditors during a bank failure, the government could be subject to the tax if the bank's foreign assets were thereby re-categorized as official foreign reserves due to the government guarantee and bailout.

Imagine if the Europeans had adopted a similar policy for the euro. The Southern European countries could have imposed a tax on Northern European countries for their excessive trade surplus financed by their banks with implicit government guarantees and explicit bank deposit guarantees. It is unlikely that the Northern European banks would have then lent so excessively to Southern Europe and the systemic risk of the European debt crisis would have been significantly reduced.

If a foreign government kept their official foreign reserves in custodial accounts outside of the deficit countries being hurt, holding the country that has custody of the assets responsible for paying the tax by withholding principal and interest payments would solve this problem.

Finally, a Nash Equilibrium states that no country alone can change policy without a loss in utility. If the U.S. was viewed as a rogue state and sanctioned, then the U.S. would have to choose whether to escalate or capitulate.

A tax on the portion of official foreign reserves that finance trade deficits is more fair and efficient with fewer side effects than competitively devaluing your currency through quantitative easing and eventually a debt crisis. If there are political calls for a wealth tax to reduce inequality, the wealth tax should be on the portion of official foreign reserves that finance trade imbalances rather than on individuals.

The U.S. has the largest economy in the world. If the U.S. decided to lead with a policy that enforced fair trade, the rest of the world would most likely go along with it in order to maintain access to the U.S. economy. Other countries would most likely adopt the policy as well to protect their own interests. After widespread adoption, the playing field for trade would have a stable convex surface, much like that marble in a bowl, and trade balance could be restored without the need to print excessive amounts of money or punish the middle class.

The Inflation Alternative

An alternative policy is for the U.S. to continue to run government budget deficits with spending targeting the symptoms. The Federal Reserve can monetize the debt much like it has been doing with quantitative easing and devalue the U.S. dollar. This policy risks distorting the U.S. economy, creating additional bad investments, increasing financial repression with ultra-low interest rates, and instigating inflationary demands. With each country trying to weaken their currency and increase financial repression, the global economy risks a currency war.

The more indebted the government becomes, the higher the risk of an economic crisis. The more unproductive the U.S. investments become to generate government and housing led growth, the slower the economy will grow and the higher unemployment and inflation will become. As inflationary demands eventually develop combined with excess bank reserves in the system, the Federal Reserve will have to raise interest rates or reserve requirements to counter the inflationary demands. Raising reserve requirements to promote government and housing debt financed by quantitative easing could lead to capital flight. Raising interest rates could force the U.S. economy into a severe recession or depression.

An inflationary policy is typically endorsed by governments around the world because it benefits excessive government spending. However, perhaps there is another group of leaders, 250 years after the Continental Congress, who are willing to be unconventional, unite their citizens rather than blame them, and tax the portion of official foreign reserves that finance trade deficits.

In this chapter a policy is proposed of taxing the portion of official foreign reserves that finance trade imbalances as an alternative to an inflationary arms race. It would restore sovereignty to any country that desired a stable economy, government, and currency. By taxing only the government financing of trade deficits, this policy does not punish trade or capital flows. The international financial system of trade would have a stable convex surface where deviations from balanced trade would induce a return to balanced trade. This policy would enhance global economic cooperation and foster sustainable growth.

Chapter 8 – Business and Government Investment

In typical political debates, there is a usually a discussion about expanding business investment and the role of government. How much should business and governments invest? Why is investment weak? When is government crowding out the private sector? This chapter discusses some of these issues from the perspective of the profit frame.

Business Investment and Uncertainty

The previous chapters illustrated how currency manipulation is playing a larger than assumed role in preventing business from investing in the U.S. Uncertainty has also played a role.

In 2011, the U.S. encountered a period of intense partisanship and brinksmanship over growing federal debt and deficits with threats to oppose further increases in the U.S. debt ceiling. As a result, Standard & Poor's downgraded the credit rating of the U.S. (United States of America Long-Term Rating Lowered To 'AA+' Due To Political Risks, Rising Debt Burden; Outlook Negative, 2011).

Since 2011 Europe finds itself in a period of great uncertainty. Europe discovered that it couldn't have an economic union in monetary policy without a political union in fiscal policy. The German elite and their bankers made loans to Southern Europe to generate economic growth in Germany, without consulting with their nation whether it was wise to lend money to countries with histories of default and political independence. Southern Europe willingly borrowed as profits were strong and optimism reigned due to the positive feedback loop that links debt growth with profits. Since 2011, however, austerity and the paradox of thrift have been in full force with cuts to spending, lower wages, shrinking bank loans, and higher taxes.

The investment options that exist when making an investment decision are called real options (Reuer & Tong, 2007). One of the most important real options is waiting for more information before investing. To make the best decision possible, businesses incorporate these real options into the value of an investment and its alternatives. These real options become more valuable with more uncertainty.

With the global economy unbalanced and the developed world facing fiscal and monetary dilemmas, the rising uncertainty makes it more difficult for business to justify investing now rather than waiting for more information about the future.

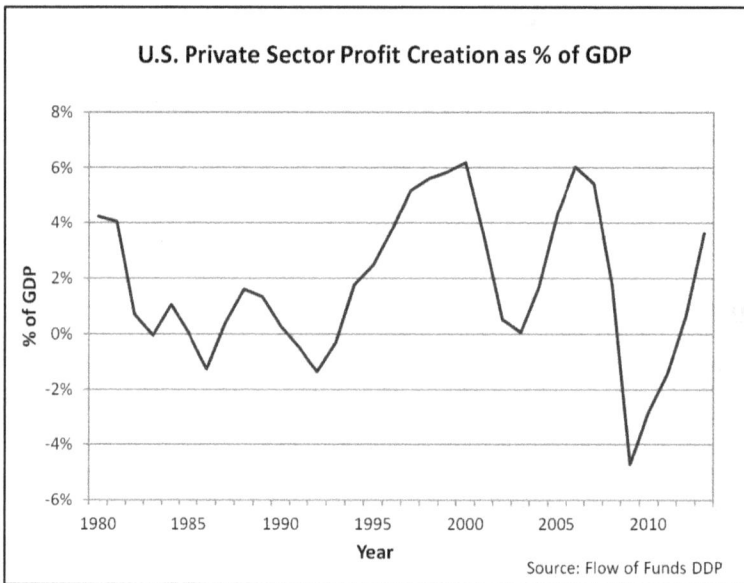

Figure 28: U.S. Private Sector Profit Creation as % of GDP

Figure 28 illustrates the U.S. private sector's contribution to profit creation since 1980. Except for the tech bubble, housing bubble, and current profit bubble, the contribution has been close to zero. Without bubbles, business has relied almost entirely on the government sector for its creation of profits. As the U.S. becomes more divided politically and economically, the uncertainty grows. Reducing the volatility of this roller-coaster ride and restoring private sector profit creation would encourage businesses investment.

A Dangerous Escape

The U.S. needs to find a path in which trade is balanced, business invests more in the U.S., and government deficits shrink. The perils of this transition range from the potential for excessive profit bubbles and inflation to outright depression. The road is treacherous because of the link between profits and debt growth.

The U.S. federal government has a deficit problem and a brewing debt problem. The U.S. federal debt is approaching 100% of GDP, although debt held by the public is significantly lower at 67% of GDP (Debt to the Penny, 2012). However, in a little over 20 years from now the debt held by the public is projected to rise from 67% of GDP to 190% of GDP (CBO 2011 Long-Term Budget Outlook, 2011). Growth begins to slow once a government's debt exceeds around 100% of GDP (Reinhart & Rogoff, This Time is Different, 2011).

One peril on the road to economic prosperity is what if the government deficit is reduced too soon or too quickly? Unless business investment and mortgage debt replaces the government deficit reduction, the amount of profits in the U.S. economy would be reduced as well. This is referred to as the "paradox of thrift" (Paradox of thrift, 2012). The reduction in profits would severely punish the stock market, home prices, and the U.S. consumer's confidence. Investors' demand for money would skyrocket and their demand for risk would plummet. It would become more difficult to employ people and take risk.

The Federal Reserve would be limited in their power. Traditional monetary policy can only motivate profit creation. It is the government and private sector which must actually borrow the money and spend it in the domestic economy to create profits. With quantitative easing, the Federal Reserve could buy existing assets from the private sector rather than new debt but it would still be up to the private sector to take a financial risk and spend their previous years' savings in a weak domestic economy to create profits.

Another peril is what if the U.S. creates too much debt growth and profits. The U.S. government has continued to run trillion dollar deficits financed by quantitative easing alongside rising business investment and mortgage debt. Consequently, a post-crisis profit bubble has been inflated. While rising profits sound nice, they will eventually have to be deflated and it could damage the U.S. politically and economically. A 50% reduction in U.S. profits from 8% of GDP to 4% of GDP could make business more reluctant to invest if they believe we are on a perpetual economic roller-coaster of uncertainty.

Crowding Out

When governments want to increase their investment spending, they confront the issue of whether they are crowding out private sector investment (Taylor, 2010). To understand this issue, the sources of financing profits will be examined to understand when the government is crowding out and when it is not.

The five sources of financing profits were described previously as

- Vendor Financing
- Dividend Recycling
- Bank Credit
- Central Bank Monetization
- Official Foreign Reserves/Foreign Lending

In this analysis, only Bank Credit and Central Bank Monetization are relevant. Vendor Financing and Dividend Recycling relate to interactions between the business and household sectors. Government investment has little impact on these decisions.

Official Foreign Reserves/Foreign lending also does not play a role in crowding out because this lending exists only for the purpose of financing trade deficits. The government may compensate for lost profits by making government investments but financing trade deficits does not limit the domestic supply of credit because it only involves foreign lenders.

U.S. Bank Credit totals approximately 60% of GDP (Figure 15). Bank Credit uses the money multiplier effect to become a source of financing profits. To maintain a ratio of 60%, Bank Credit must grow at the same rate as nominal GDP. Business and government investment compete for this limited resource. Access to bank credit is one of the areas where crowding out can occur.

Central Bank Monetization is a source of financing profits that can actually increase the supply of money and bank credit available for government investment. The major constraint for Central Bank Monetization is inflation. When inflation reaches levels higher than central bank targets, the central bank must limit debt growth and subsequently access to Bank Credit.

Government investment also has the potential to crowd out consumer spending. Note that when government investments are financed by household savings, this does not generate profits immediately. The government spending cancels out with the household savings. The net result is that instead of getting household spending, an economy gets government investment. Most emerging market countries like China have adopted this model in order to make the infrastructure and educational investments to propel faster growth rates. However, this form of crowding out only works if the government investments are productive and enable faster growth and profits in the future.

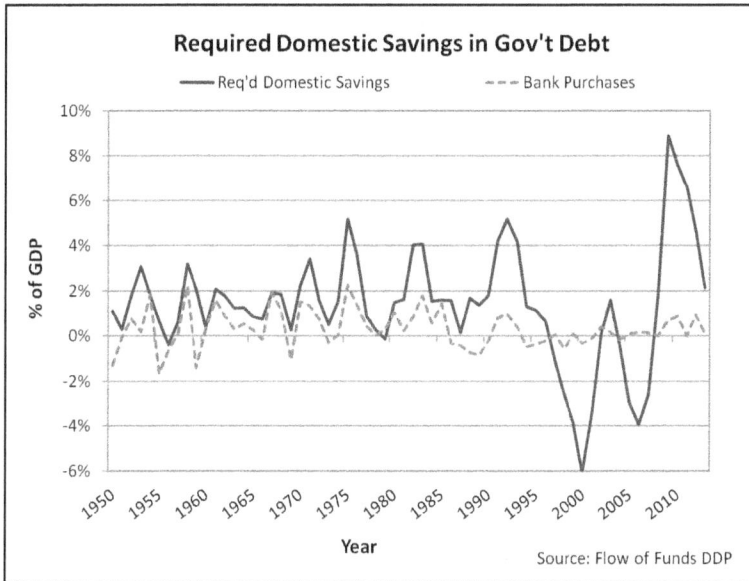

Figure 29: Required Domestic Savings in Government Debt

Figure 29 illustrates that since the S&L crisis in the early 1990s crowding out has not been an issue in the U.S. thanks to quantitative easing. The Required Domestic Savings line once again is defined for our purposes as the difference between the government budget deficit and the trade deficit (if any) to reflect the amount of domestic savings required to finance the government. With large trade deficits and bubbles, foreign lenders have easily financed government budget deficits. After the financial crisis of 2008, quantitative easing, which is Central Bank Monetization, has financed government budget deficits to prevent any crowding out or rise in interest rates.

However, on the road to economic prosperity, this debate will eventually be resurrected once quantitative easing stops filling the gap. If the U.S. government wants to increase its investment in infrastructure, it will have to come at the expense of entitlement spending, household spending, or business investment. Bank Credit is limited if a profit bubble or excess inflation is to be avoided and the government will have to make choices.

As of 2013, Europe is in a period of austerity with limited Central Bank Monetization and declining bank credit (ECB, 2013). Yet even with additional monetization, it is unclear whether it would lead to more business investment and job growth without structural reforms like promoting competition within the workforce. Quantitative easing can slow down deleveraging but if the banking system must shrink as a percent of the economy, the loss in growth potential is unavoidable. The European Central Bank (ECB) is under pressure to reduce the pain that a deleveraging involves but deleveraging is unavoidably painful.

Economists are also debating whether Asia has reached the end of the road with their economic model based on crowding out household spending. The growth in real estate lending and shadow bank products worries analysts (Das, 2014). China must structurally reform if the productivity of their government investments is diminishing and doesn't enable faster growth in the future. If so, rising inflation or a debt crisis in China will signal when the decline in productivity is terminal and China has to find a better economic model. In an economy controlled by government it is usually inflation that is the canary in the coal mine.

In this chapter we saw how rising uncertainty is one of the consequences of trade imbalances. Without quantitative easing, the economic roller-coaster is much more violent and government must compete with business for a limited amount of bank credit. Even if the U.S. is able to reduce currency manipulation and get off the economic roller-coaster, the road to economic prosperity may be treacherous if the transition from government deficits to business investment is not managed wisely.

Chapter 9 - Tax Policy

This chapter explores some of the different kinds of taxes that businesses and individuals face that are not typically discussed. The inflation tax, the limited liability tax rate, and investment option tax are embedded in the tax code and largely invisible, but are important to business investment. The remainder of the chapter examines a hodgepodge of issues that are related to taxes. How progressive should the tax structure be? Does taxation encourage philanthropy? Is it time for a federal consumption tax? Should the estate tax be replaced? What are the keys to a successful subsidy program?

The Inflation Tax

Inflation is a tax on wealth. It is like a consumption tax in that it taxes everyone but it is more skewed towards the saver since it targets financial savings more than spending. Governments and their central banks usually target a certain level of inflation. The Federal Reserve targets an inflation rate around 2% per year (Longer-Run Goals and Policy Strategy, 2012). They target a rate greater than zero because it is believed to be easier for businesses to raise wages more slowly when their employees lag average productivity than trying to obtain wage reductions.

When a government is not able to tax its citizens with other forms of taxation, it can resort to monetization or printing money to pay its bills. In this case, inflation is a source of tax revenue. The underlying issue in the European crisis for a country like Greece is - do they have the operational capability to tax their citizens? There are clear benefits for Greece to stay in the Euro currency. If Greece can collect taxes from their citizens, they can lower their budget deficits and comply with the austerity requirements. However, if the government is so dysfunctional that it is not able to collect the required taxes from its citizens, then Greece will need an inflation rate greater than the rest of the Europe and must exit the Euro currency in order to achieve this higher inflation rate.

Inflation creates illusory capital gains to owners of capital. In recognition of these illusory gains, capital gains tax rates are usually lower than ordinary income tax rates. Some policymakers have proposed indexing capital gains to inflation to avoid taxing these illusory gains. If capital gains were indexed to inflation, then capital gains income could be treated like any other ordinary income. Indexing would also treat individuals equally regardless of the rate of return earned on the investment or the holding period of the investment.

Table 9 : Calculating the Inflation Tax Rate

LT Capital Gains Tax Rate	Before 2013 15%	After 2013 24%	Moderate Inflation 24%
Pretax Return	5%	5%	10%
Inflation Rate	2.4%	2.4%	7.4%
Real Return	2.6% (5% - 2.4%)	2.6% (5% - 2.4%)	2.6% (10% - 7.4%)
Tax Due	0.75% (15% x 5%)	1.2% (24% x 5%)	2.4% (24% x 10%)
Real After-Tax Return	1.85% (2.6% - 0.75%)	1.4% (2.6% - 1.2%)	0.2% (2.6% - 2.4%)
Real Tax Rate	28.85% (0.75% / 2.6%)	46.15% (1.2% / 2.6%)	92.31% (2.4% / 2.6%)
Commentary	In line with Ordinary Tax Rates	Taxing Capital more than Labor	Wealth Destruction
Inflation Tax Rate	13.85% (28.85% - 15%)	22.15% (46.15% - 24%)	68.31% (92.31% - 24%)

Since the U.S. does not index capital gains to inflation, it is possible to compute the U.S. inflation tax rate for a variety of holding periods and rates of return.

The first two scenarios in Table 9 assume an investor earns a 5% annual return that matches the desired growth rate in nominal GDP. Both the real GDP growth rate and the real return are 2.6%. Real GDP growth is nominal GDP growth excluding inflation. A real return is a rate of return after subtracting inflation.

Table 9 illustrates that the inflation tax effectively doubles the capital gains tax rate when inflation is only 2.4%. With inflation at 7.4% and a 2.6% real return, the inflation tax now effectively destroys investment growth unless you have been given a politically-connected tax break.

The differences between the first two scenarios in Table 9 reflect the changes in the tax rates after passage of the Affordable Care Act. With the effective capital gains tax rate raised from 15% to 24% to reflect a 20% long-term capital gains tax rate plus a 4% Medicare surcharge, then what looks like an 9% increase in the tax rate is actually a 17.3% increase in the real income tax rate from 29% to 46%, almost double the 9% increase.

Also note that the real income tax rate in the second scenario of 46% becomes larger than the tax rate on wage income. If you want less of something, tax it more. A 46% federal tax rate, not counting state and local taxes, is a bad sign for future business investment and capital mobility unless government acknowledges the inflation tax and adopts policies to mitigate it. The higher the inflation tax becomes, the higher the required rate of return must be for investors to finance projects and for business owners to hire new employees.

In the third scenario of Table 9 an investor is assumed to earn a 10% annual return that matches nominal GDP growth of 10% in an inflationary environment of 7.4%. The real GDP growth rate and the real return are still 2.6%. However, now the real tax rate on capital becomes confiscatory and destructive at 92.13%. It doesn't take much inflation before investors are incentivized to preserve their capital by taking it out of a country and investing it elsewhere. Rising inflation is a precursor to capital flight. Figure 30 and Figure 31 illustrate how the holding period and inflation rate can significantly affect the real capital gains tax rate after adjusting for inflation.

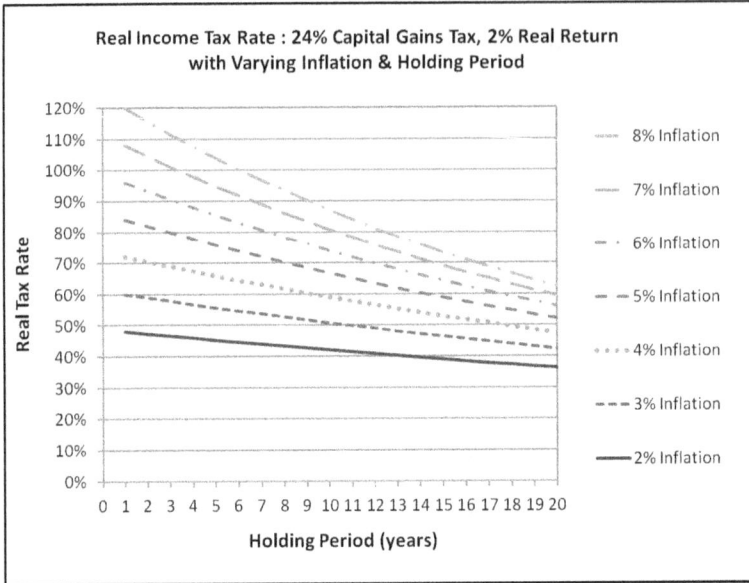

Figure 30: 2% Real Return - Capital Gains with Inflation Tax Rate

Figure 30 uses a 2% pretax real return as a desired real return for a fixed income investor. Figure 31 uses a 5% pretax real return as a desired real return for an equity investor.

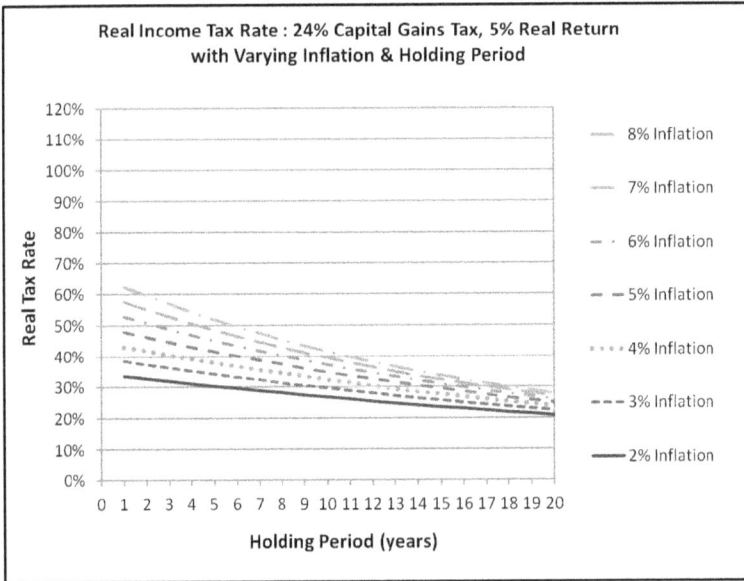

Figure 31: 5% Real Return - Capital Gains with Inflation Tax

The higher inflation becomes, the larger the inflation tax becomes. This becomes a form of financial repression. Outstanding investors earning above average returns pay the lowest inflation tax.

Figure 30 clearly demonstrates how disabling and damaging inflation can become if inflation expectations are not contained. Effective tax rates can exceed 100%. The longer an investment is held, the lower the effective tax rate becomes due to compounding. This discourages capital mobility or investors' willingness to reallocate investments to other areas which slows GDP and employment growth.

Because of the damage that inflation can do to savings, U.S. pension funds and other retirement vehicles are not subject to a capital gains tax. Similarly, the U.S. government created a tax exemption for capital gains on housing as a home is the primary storage of wealth for the U.S. middle class.. The U.S. needs to move away from housing investment that is tax advantaged and move towards business investment and capital mobility that isn't excessively taxed by inflation. The U.S. economy needs a diverse set of business owners/investors that encompass more than just the tax-advantaged, centrally-planned allocators at pension funds or government investment offices.

The Limited Liability Tax

The corporation is a political entity that was created by government to facilitate employment, investment, and wealth creation. One reason why corporations have been effective in creating wealth is because the owners of corporations are provided with limited liability and able to raise capital from a large and global investor base.

Limited liability means that only the amount of capital that has been contributed to a corporation is at risk in a bankruptcy (Reitzel, Lyden, Roberts, & Severance, 1990). A creditor is not allowed to seek reimbursement from the owners of the company in excess of what was contributed to the corporation. In cases of fraud, however, creditors can seek compensation. In the U.S. judicial system, failure has not been considered a crime and thus owners of corporations are able to pursue investments with a variety of risk profiles. This limited liability feature has value much like an option which protects the buyer from losses over a certain threshold. It is reasonable to assume that the government would want to tax this benefit.

There are two types of corporations in the U.S. S Corporations are typically small business corporations that are limited to no more than 100 U.S. tax-resident owners. S Corporations can pass through their income to their individual owners without a corporate income tax and still obtain the benefit of limited liability. C Corporations are typically larger corporations that are not limited to 100 owners and can raise capital from foreign individuals or entities. C Corporations are subject to corporate income taxes. The ability to raise capital from a diverse set of investors also has value to a corporation; however, it is unclear why the government would want to tax this diversity.

In determining the "effective" tax rate for an individual shareholder of a C corporation, one should include both the corporate income tax rate as well as the dividend income tax rate to individual shareholders. Governments not only tax a C corporation's income but also typically tax any dividend income the C corporation transfers to its shareholders or owners. A dividend is a transfer of accumulated earnings from a corporation to its owners in the form of cash. The effective tax rate is useful for comparing tax burdens on small businesses that are not politically connected across many different countries.

Table 10: Limited Liability Tax Scenarios

Example	Limited Liability (C Corp)	Unlimited Liability (Individual)	Suggested Limited Liability Treatment
Pre-Tax Profit	$100	$100	$100
Corporate Tax Rate	35%		25%
After-Tax Profit	$65	$100	$75
Individual Tax Rate (Dividend or AMT)	Average Dividend Rate 18.8%	Average Ordinary Rate 28%	Average Dividend Rate 17%
Owner Proceeds	$52.78	$72.00	$62.25
Limited Liability Tax Rate	**19.22%** (72-52.78)	Unlimited Liability	**9.75%** (72-62.25)

A typical federal tax situation in the U.S. is illustrated in the left column of Table 10. Taking into account the tax brackets for 2013, the average corporate tax rate is represented as 35% and the average dividend income tax rate for individuals is represented as 18.8%. When combined the maximum federal "effective" marginal tax rate is 47.22%. The middle column of Table 10 assumes a typical U.S. sole proprietorship or partnership has an average ordinary tax rate of 28%. With these assumptions, the U.S. federal tax code imposes a limited liability tax rate of 19.22% on C corporations.

The combined corporate income tax rate and dividend tax rate should be higher than the sole proprietorship alternatives to reflect the value of the limited liability option. A zero or negative limited liability tax rate ignores the value of the limited liability. On the other hand, a large limited liability tax rate on C corporations punishes the entities that create most of the jobs in the U.S. economy. A limited liability tax rate around 8% to 10% seems like a reasonable compromise.

In the past when individual tax rates were higher than corporate tax rates, the limited liability tax rate was negative. Income and wealth were held in corporations and other tax-advantaged entities rather than transferred to shareholders in order to avoid the high tax rates and double taxation. When pundits refer to historically high tax rates in the U.S. or Sweden as being harmless, they are ignoring the fact that income and wealth was not generated in the entities that were heavily taxed but rather in the legal entities that were reasonably taxed. Corporations used to provide perks to their employees rather than pay bonuses that would be taxed away.

Today, businesses have many more global options available to them than in the past. Corporations routinely transfer profits to low-tax countries or entities. For the U.S. to encourage domestic business investment it needs to consider not only the tax rates of all its legal entities but also the tax rates of its global competitors. Businesses will move profits to the lowest form of taxation available.

Adopting a globally competitive business tax rate and reducing the limited liability tax rate to 8% to 10% could unlock and encourage the business investment that the U.S. needs in order to return to a stable source of profits and growth.

The Investment Option Tax

The U.S. government also owns a tax option on business investment. If a business invests in a profitable project, the business will owe a tax to the government. However, if the project is not profitable, the business can only get a deduction for the loss if it has other business income to offset the loss. It can carry forward, or sometimes backwards, the loss to deduct against future or past income but the business must have some offsetting income. This is like "heads I win, tails you lose". If a business succeeds, the government acts like a partner but if a business fails, it is no longer your partner to share in the loss.

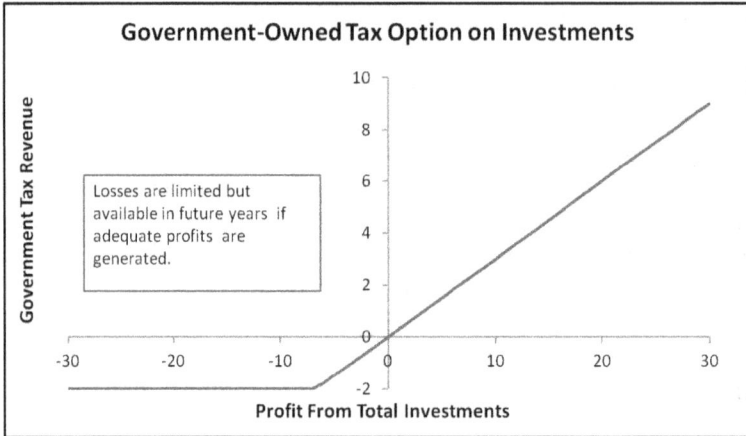

Figure 32: Government-Owned Tax Option on Investments

The payoff to the government is like owning an option (Figure 32). The higher the tax rate, the more valuable the government's option is. The larger the uncertainty in the investment, the more valuable the government's option is. The private sector is short this option. They are forced to sell this option to the government to the extent that they are not diversified. The cost of this option raises the hurdle rate for new investments because when uncertainty is included in an investment analysis, the potential asymmetry of the after-tax payoff reduces the expected return. If the tax rate is set too high, the government-owned tax option forces businesses to diversify, reduce their investment risk, or increase their hurdle rate all of which slows growth and job creation.

In order to encourage U.S. investment, the cost of the investment option tax should be minimized. The lower the business tax rate, the less the option costs. Tax loopholes not only forego government revenue but also require higher tax rates to compensate for the lost revenue and increases the investment option tax. Therefore, business tax rates should be as low as possible and applied broadly without loopholes.

The Consumption Tax

In the U.S., the labor participation rate has been declining since 2000 and is expected to continue to decline to around 60% over the next two decades (Figure 33).

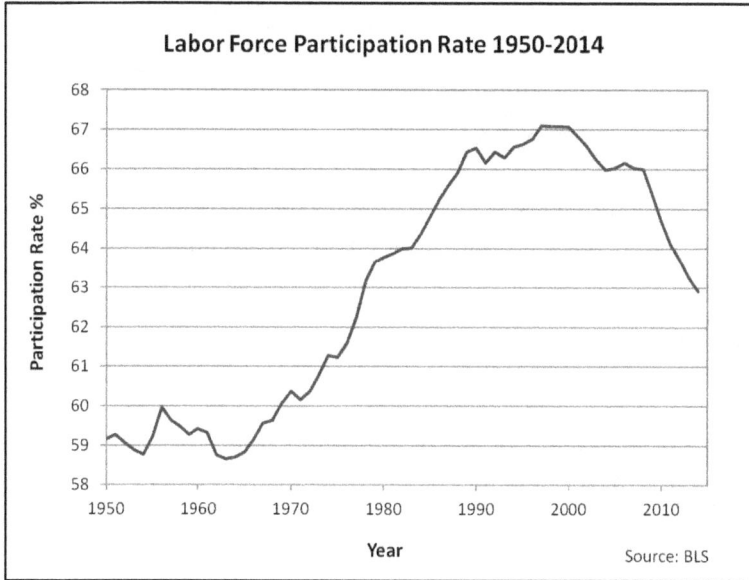

Figure 33: Labor Force Participation Rate

One consequence of the declining labor participation rate is that the income tax base of the U.S. government narrows as less people are working and paying taxes to support the government. A consumption tax as a complement to a lower income tax rate could help broaden the tax base and would require retiring individuals to continue to support the federal government in proportion to their spending.

Table 11: Examples of State Sales Tax (Sales Tax Institute, 2012)

State	Sales Tax Rate
New Jersey	7.000%
California	6.250%
Texas	6.250%
Florida	6.000%
Ohio	5.500%
New York	4.000%

A consumption tax is widely used to finance state and local governments. A sales tax is an example of a consumption tax. Rather than taxing income as an individual or corporation receives it, a consumption tax taxes an individual or business' income when they spend it. Table 11 provides some examples of state sales tax rates in the U.S (Sales Tax Institute, 2012).

Some groups refer to a proposal for only a consumption tax as the Fair Tax and there is a growing movement to consider a national sales tax as a source of revenue for the U.S. federal government (The Fair Tax Plan, 2012).

One of the benefits or disadvantages of a consumption tax, depending on your political view, is it gives the government the opportunity to establish a broader tax base. A broader tax base means that a larger portion of the population or wealth is taxed. For example, a consumption tax can tax a wealthy retiree with minimal income based on their level of spending. A consumption tax can also tax a portion of the black market and individuals or entities that can misstate their income but not their spending. If applied to investment spending, the consumption tax would also tax a corporation undertaking business investment and job creation as well as a business that has minimal taxable income due to tax exemptions and deductions.

To overcome the regressive nature of a consumption tax (regressive meaning that lower income individuals pay a larger share of their income in taxes), proponents have advocated a fixed rebate amount to be paid to every household annually (Fair Tax, 2012). Proponents also argue that by broadening the tax base and lowering the tax on work, a rising tide would lift all boats and all segments of the country would benefit (Gale, Burman, & Suarez, 2005).

Opponents argue that even with a rebate a consumption tax is still regressive because high-income households could still see a lower tax bill unless business investment is taxed as well. High-income households spend a lower portion of their income and thus could pay a smaller percent of their income in taxes. For example, income that is invested in tangible assets like gold or undeveloped land could escape a consumption tax. Similarly, income spent while abroad and foreign investments could also escape a consumption tax.

However, income that is reinvested in other people rather than taxed does not mean a consumption tax is necessarily regressive when one looks through the investment. This issue will be investigated next when we discuss how progressive the income tax system should be. A consumption tax with a rebate has an ability to substitute for a portion of income taxes without making the tax code more regressive.

Whether a consumption tax would encourage savings and investment would depend on the policy details. If a consumption tax were used in place of an income tax, it would surely encourage savings but it could equally discourage investment if capital investments are also taxed. If capital investments were exempt from the consumption tax, it would surely favor savings and investment over consumption.

As the workforce of the U.S. ages and retires in greater number, the federal government will be under increasing pressure to consider a consumption tax as a source of revenue to broaden its tax base.

The Marginal Utility Tax Rate

In "American Gridlock", Woody Brock examined several theories of fairness and redistribution of wealth (Brock, 2012) using game theory. Three different government structures were analyzed with a 2-stage super game. In the first stage of the game, a country decides a constitution upfront with a set of rules, taxes, and incentives and in the second stage, they live their lives. The goal is to optimize the sum of everyone's utility or life, liberty, and the pursuit of happiness. The results illustrate the conflict between tax redistribution and private investment.

In the first government structure, the citizens of the game believe they are certain to live in poverty and just hope to achieve the poverty level when they live their lives. They don't believe they will ever rise above the poverty level so there is no value assigned above the poverty line. With this certain despair, the solution of the super game suggests an extremely progressive tax rates. This system accurately describes the communist system in which everyone is poor and they are certain of their future poverty.

In the second government structure, the citizens do not know how well they will do in their lives but they all have the same economic resources to succeed. It allows for inequality but assumes equal opportunity. The second-stage game suggests a "redistribution" to meet the basic needs of its citizens due to the theory of diminishing marginal return. According to the theory of diminishing marginal return, the poor would obtain a greater happiness from a redistributed dollar than if the rich person kept it. However, it recognizes that excessive "redistribution" will lower the happiness of everyone.

The third government structure is similar to the second government structure just discussed that included equal opportunity; however, it removes threats and coalitions from the game. By simplifying the game in this way, the outcome is similar to the second government structure but the system is now theoretically able to meet the basic needs of all its citizens. This is an ivory tower theoretical world because threats and coalitions are abundant in the real world.

From these three alternative government structures, the theory suggests that the amount of redistribution should depend on the certainty of poverty, the realization of equal opportunity, a diminishing marginal utility function, and possibly the abundance of threats and coalitions. These are some of the biggest issues at the heart of the debate around economic fairness.

How certain is our future poverty? The U.S. has always fostered optimism and the power of the individual. The "American Dream" is a manifestation of this optimism. The U.S. became the strongest country in the world by believing in its citizens through not only democracy but also decentralized business investment. As communism revealed, taking away hope is a powerful punishment for an economy. A government policy that goes beyond meeting the basic needs of its citizens and damages the optimism of the country is a government policy failure.

What about equal opportunity? In the U.S., both Democrats and Republicans believe in equal opportunity. While this belief is strong in both parties, its implementation is debated in every election. Republicans believe equal opportunity is achieved through effort. Opportunity is there if one makes the effort to find it. Republicans talk about the entrepreneur and the small business person who dedicates long hours to make a business succeed and grow an economy for everyone. In this viewpoint, nobody is denied the opportunity to try and persevere. Democrats believe that some individuals need assistance so they can have the opportunity to make that effort. Government resources are necessary to overcome the obstacles. Democrats talk about the economic potential that could be achieved if more government resources were devoted to the cause.

Threats and coalitions can be seen in many places in the U.S. The cartels of industries, unions, and governments are coalitions that distort outcomes. Lobbyists limit growth by advocating benefits, economic stimulus, and tax loopholes rather than balanced trade and broader, lower tax rates. These coalitions make it more difficult to meet the basic needs of the vulnerable.

The two government structures that assumed equal opportunity suggest "redistribution" based on the theory of diminishing marginal returns. In economics, happiness is called utility. Economists typically use utility functions to model preferences. A log function is one possible function that satisfies the law of diminishing marginal return. In a *ln(1+ax)* function, every doubling of the input variable generates the same percentage increase in utility.

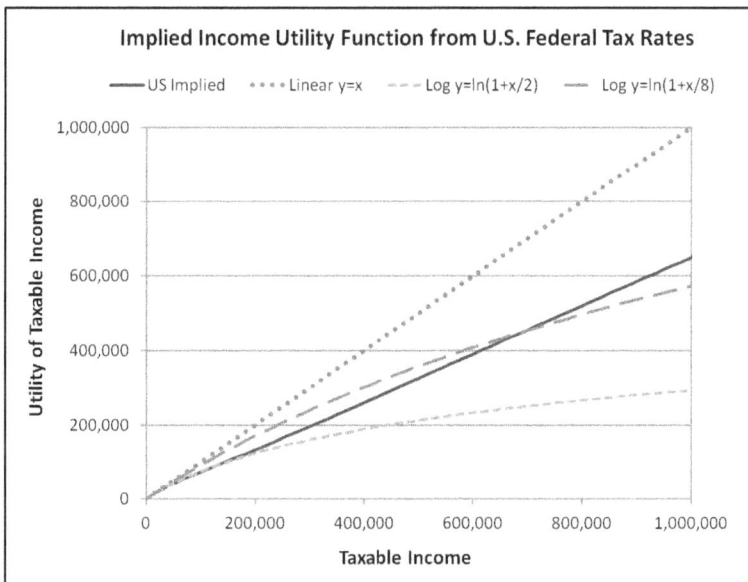

Figure 34: Implied Income Utility Function for US Federal Tax Rates

Figure 34 compares the U.S. individual tax code's implied utility function with two log utility functions. Because the top U.S. federal tax rate in 2013 is constant for incomes above $400K, the tax code's marginal utility no longer diminishes above $400K. If a log function $y = ln(1 + x/2)$ is used to approximate the implied utility function for typical

U.S. incomes under $100,000, it doesn't take much income before the log function suggests confiscatory tax rates of 70% or more. Using a log function $y = ln(1 + x/8)$ that tries to fit implied tax rates for incomes approaching $1 million is more reasonable but suggests tax rates around 5% for most people and 15% for taxable income of $250K. This function eventually recommends 70% confiscatory tax rates at incomes approaching $4 million.

However, the theory of diminishing marginal utility does not suggest that taxation is the best and only form of "redistribution". Perhaps, marginal tax rates should not be as progressive as suggested by a simple diminishing marginal utility curve because taxes and private investment are substitutes and both accomplish redistribution.

As incomes rise, so does savings and investments. A person who saves and invests in other people is essentially deferring or diminishing their "utility" voluntarily. Savings is like stored utility. While income used for consumption can be assumed to benefit only the person spending the money, investment is an organizational undertaking creating jobs and wages for its employees. The marginal utility of wealth should be based on how it changes the utility of every person affected by the savings and investments. A proper marginal utility curve should _look through_ the investments and recognize that almost all of the benefit or utility accrues to the workers.

As Peter Drucker explained in Post-Capitalist Society, Karl Marx was wrong in predicting the collapse of capitalism because he assumed that all of the gains in productivity would accrue to the capitalist. In fact, almost all of the gains have accrued to the worker in the form of a higher standard of living and more leisure (Drucker, 1993).

Once it is realized that wealthy people voluntarily save and invest, the diminishing marginal utility curve does not imply what tax rates should be but rather what a combination of tax rates plus investment rates should be. Since both taxes and investment act similarly in reducing consumption, the subject of taxes on the wealthy becomes an issue of who are the best stewards of wealth as Andrew Carnegie wrote in what is referred to as the Gospel of Wealth (Carnegie, 1889).

If both government spending and private investment achieve the same productivity gains and increase in utility, citizens should be indifferent between government investment and private investment. However, when redistributed government tax revenues are spent on items that fail to increase the overall happiness of its citizens as much as private investment would, then tax redistribution slows economic growth with good investments taken away and replaced with inferior investments.

Private investment and tax redistribution are like partners. Both help meet the basic needs of a country. Both should play to their strengths. Government should focus on areas where private investment and job creation cannot go, such as supporting the truly disabled and elderly or where there are free rider issues such as defense. Government should insure a stable, sustainable environment for investment. A government that preempts business and private investment through high tax rates, unbalanced trade, and unaccountable redistribution is most likely creating a situation where productivity slows and growth in the standard of living becomes more difficult to generate unless the country can ride on the coattails of larger countries.

If the trade-off between tax redistribution and private investment is a function of stewardship, then the tax rates on the rich should be a function of their investing intelligence. If the rich are inferior investors compared to the middle class, then taxing the rich benefits society. On the other hand, if the rich are better investors than the middle class, then taxing the rich reduces the potential of a country. Most likely, the rich are no smarter or dumber than the middle class. Therefore, it is probably optimal that the tax rate is flat after a certain income level in which savings is a reasonable portion of income. Any concern over lack of competition can be controlled by government antitrust regulation.

Another reason why tax rates may not be as progressive as the diminishing marginal utility curve suggests is because tax rates must compete with other countries and with other domestic legal entities like corporations. There may not be a difference in the theoretical models between giving and taking but there is a perceived difference in the real world. Taxes are enforced by police power and paid to avoid the threat of fines or imprisonment. Investing and charity are giving. If private investment and charitable giving achieve the same or better outcomes for society as a whole, it is better to encourage private investment and charitable giving in order to stay competitive.

Finally, a Bayesian approach that recognizes that past wealth creation from an entrepreneur might foster additional entrepreneurial wealth creation might suggest a less progressive tax system to encourage future entrepreneurial investments that benefit everyone.

How steep should the progressive tax system be and when will it start to punish everyone and not just the wealthy? The optimism of its citizens is probably the best guide. The more obstacles that citizens must overcome to succeed, the less optimistic they will be and more unlikely to invest and raise their standard of living. The perceived moral difference between giving and taking may also affect the optimism of individuals and their willingness to make an effort.

Measuring optimism is different than measuring confidence because optimism incorporates luck. It may be that the wealthy got lucky or they "didn't build that" (Obama, 2012). A theoretical capitalist system has "complete markets" where you can buy insurance on anything (Brock, 2012). Would the wealthy have hedged their bets if they could have? In the real world, luck is at the heart of optimism and making an effort. Immigrants uprooted their lives and came to the U.S. for the opportunity to be lucky. It is important that a progressive tax system does not go too far by taking away optimism and luck and replacing them with the certainty of poverty.

The Urban Tax

Because urban cities tend to have a higher tax burden, they are more sensitive to federal taxes. If a New York City investor paid a 15% federal capital gains tax and an 11% state and city tax on $1 of investment income, the 11% state and city tax acts like a 12.9% tax on the $0.85 remaining after federal tax (e.g., 0.11/0.85). If the federal capital gains tax rate rises to 24%, the 11% tax now acts like a 14.5% tax on the $0.76 remaining after federal tax. Thus, even though the state and local income tax rate did not change, the incentive to avoid the urban tax rose. For investments that include the inflation tax as well, the incentive to avoid the urban tax could be even larger rising to over 20% ($0.11 / $0.54). It is not a coincidence that the urban cities of the U.S. began a renaissance when inflation and the U.S. federal tax rates were lowered in the 1980's. If the U.S. returns to the high federal tax rates and inflation of the 1970's, its cities may once again decline as capital investment is withheld and allocated elsewhere.

The Charitable Deduction

A tax system should be neutral towards charity. Government should not punish or limit charitable giving as this is what totalitarian governments do in order to weaken their competitors and foster control. Nor should charitable giving come at the expense of the public good. Tax policy is more neutral when donors only achieve income tax benefits associated with the cost basis of their donation rather than its full value.

In the U.S., charitable giving is an alternative to paying a capital gains tax or an estate tax. If donations are given in the form of highly appreciated assets that haven't been taxed already, the decision to give is nearly unaffected by taxes or tax rates. The avoidance of tax simply looks like a matching grant program from the donor's point of view. A donor could realize capital gains, pay the capital gains tax, and give the remainder to the organization receiving the gift. By allowing the donor to avoid capital gain taxes, the government essentially matches the gift in proportion to the tax rate. Because tax exempt organizations generally do not have to pay tax on their investment income, the donation can also be thought of as having been transferred to the tax-exempt organization from the very beginning when it was worth its cost basis (i.e., as if held by the tax-exempt organization the whole time).

The tax code should ensure a deduction for charitable giving regardless of the income of the donor. This deduction should equal the cost basis of the donation but no more. This would promote charitable giving and place non-profit organizations as alternatives to government without harming the public good that relies on tax revenues to provide basic services.

The Estate or Death Tax

In the U.S., a considerable amount of effort is put into minimizing the estate tax which is a tax due after death. Public opinion varies on the tax depending on the information available and the frame used in polling (Sides, 2011).

One of the most relevant features of the estate tax is that it doesn't tax capital gains. The cost basis of an investment is irrelevant in the determination of the tax. It is only the value at the time of death that matters. The reason for this is because the estate tax can be viewed as an alternative to the capital gains tax. Most small businesses are never sold so capital gain taxes are never due. Steve Jobs didn't pay tax on the vast majority of his gains in Apple stock because he didn't sell. The estate tax is designed to tax these capital gains in addition to wealth.

The estate tax is more like a capital mobility tax. If an individual subject to the estate tax decides to sell a profitable investment and realize a large capital gain, the after-tax proceeds will still be subject to the estate tax. In order to avoid the double taxation, individuals tend to hold or donate profitable investments rather than allocate capital to more productive purposes. After receiving the donation, the non-profit organization can reallocate capital.

The U.S. would be economically more efficient if it replaced the estate tax with a capital gains tax upon death. This would eliminate the capital mobility penalty and allow capital to move to where it can generate the greatest growth. Replacing the estate tax with a capital gains tax would also more accurately tax the gains that the government is trying to capture; from those who never sold.

For the portion of the estate tax that is wealth related, the only real concern the government should have about wealth is whether it becomes too concentrated. However, the history of philanthropy has proven that this is not a concern. Most of the richest people in U.S. history, from John D. Rockefeller to Bill Gates, have donated the vast proportion of their wealth to charitable and public causes. Taxing wealth relies on the same arguments as a progressive tax system. Only if the wealthy are incompetent investors is it in the public interest to tax their income a second time under the estate tax.

Labor mobility and capital mobility are keys to private sector investment. They both revolve around freedom to choose. It is important that government policy does not hinder these choices or distort the outcomes too much. The estate tax is a poor proxy to the goals it seeks to achieve. A capital gains tax at death would be a much more effective substitute in growing the economy and meeting the basic needs of the citizens with minimal effects on philanthropy.

The Subsidy Tax

Governments believe that subsidies are a valuable tool for providing opportunity to all of its citizens. However, the evidence shows that due to their poor design and lack of perspective, subsidies typically benefit the suppliers of subsidized goods rather than the intended buyers. When witnessing the damage done, one is reminded of the 6th century Chinese strategist's advice "keep your friends close and your enemies closer" (Tzu & Griffith, 1971). Are the advocates of middle-class subsidies the friends or enemies of the middle-class? Do they not know that subsidizing the buyer while limiting supply is an exercise in futility?

Consider the mortgage interest deduction. Who did it benefit? It was created to make it easier for lower-income people to buy a home. In reality it helped the people who already owned a home, land owners, and the companies who build homes. With interest payments tax-deductible, homeowners could raise the price of their home because the home was now more affordable. As housing prices rose, lower-income families were forced to save for a larger down-payment and take greater financial risk. If the mortgage interest deduction was gradually repealed, first-time home buyers would find it easier to come up with down payments for existing houses while new home builders would face a more difficult sell. Raw land prices could fall as home builders would have to lower their costs to compete with existing housing.

Next, consider student loan subsidies. The cost of education has risen faster than inflation for several years (Higher Education Price Index, 2012). Who has benefited? The students who now graduate with large debts? The primary beneficiaries have been the schools and administrators as they pursue rankings and expand their power base. In data released by the Education Department's National Center for Education, full-time administrators in higher education have outnumbered full-time instructors since 2006 (Jaschik, 2008). Because rankings are so subjective and everyone has the potential to win, many schools overinvest or "over bundle" in their pursuit of higher rankings which raises tuitions (Mitchell, 2012).

The original reason for rising tuition given by educators was that they could not share in the productivity gains of other industries so tuition was rising relative to other products and services (Ehrenberg). Yet, the Higher Education Price Index (HEPI) clearly shows salaries of faculty and administrators outpacing inflation (Higher Education Price Index, 2012). Schools now advertize their "net pricing" which is the price difference between tuition and the subsidies.

The rise in tuition is largely a consequence of the ever rising subsidies to the buyers of education. If you want to benefit the student, the supply must go up and the cost of education must come down. For example, policies targeted to increase the supply of science programs would be beneficial. Targeted investments in education technology would be a more effective government policy than arming students with subsidies and debt. Offering a shortened "training version" of college rather than the full "education version" could assist students in obtaining the knowledge they need to succeed at a lower cost.

Finally, consider the U.S. health insurance system. The subsidies to Medicare patients and the "fee-for-service" model have meant that the U.S. pays the highest medical bills in the world (World Health Statistics, 2011). U.S. drug companies regularly charge U.S. patients more than in other countries reflecting their higher per capita income (Morgan & Hurley, 2004). The net effect is that the drug companies and healthcare suppliers benefit while the U.S. taxpayers take on a larger debt load.

Rising prices should lead to an increase in supply. However, in most of these situations, the industry is regulated and industry cartels limit the supply. For example, the American Medical Association (AMA) controls the number of medical schools in the U.S. (Brock, 2012). Schools are accredited and educators licensed. Zoning laws require new homes to typically be built in suburbs far from the city center. Government would be much more effective supporting policies that increase the supply of these goods and lower their cost.

One subsidy that is considered to have been successful was the GI Bill of Rights. This law was passed after World War II to provide veterans with low-cost mortgages, tuition and living expenses for school, one year of unemployment insurance, and loans to start businesses (Bennett, 1996). It is credited with helping build the middle class and prosperity after the war. One of the reasons it succeeded is because the subsidies were temporary. As the veterans graduated, the schools would have to replace the veterans with non-subsidized students so any increase in tuition would have to be temporary. Second, higher education changed from offering a "liberal arts education" to meeting the practical needs of its students by offering more vocational, engineering, and math courses. The nature of college changed to meet the needs of the general public rather than the elite. In this way, the supply of education increased and its cost was lowered through reform.

A lot was covered in this chapter. We examined

- How the inflation tax acts like a doubling of the capital gains tax and how destructive it can be to tax inflated gains as inflation rises.
- How the limited liability tax and the government-owned investment tax option can discourage investment.
- How the U.S. federal government may need to implement a consumption tax as the labor participation rate declines.
- How important it is to have optimism and luck in an economy when analyzing redistribution.
- How private investment and tax redistribution are substitutes and the issue becomes who are the best stewards of wealth making the wisest investments to maximize the benefit for all citizens. This can be analyzed by looking through an investment to all who benefit from it.

- How raising *federal* taxes punishes the high-tax urban areas by magnifying urban taxes and discouraging urban investment.
- How taxes are neutral to philanthropy if only the cost basis is allowed to be deducted and without regard to the income of the donor.
- How the estate tax should be replaced with a capital gains tax to avoid the capital mobility penalty and double taxation.
- How subsidizing the buyer while limiting supply is an exercise in futility.

Chapter 10 - Income Disparity

Income disparity in the U.S. has become a hot-button issue after the financial crisis of 2008. There has been growing concern over the rise in income disparity and warnings of potential instability and slow growth if it continues to rise. Like the rising postwar debt-to-GDP ratio, a closer examination of the rise in inequality helps bring light onto the effects of government and monetary policy and to what extent the increase can be reversed.

The income disparity problem is very complex and has not been definitively studied yet. This chapter explores the rise in income inequality, how it is a global phenomenon, and how global trade imbalances and its consequences affect it.

Rising Income Disparity

There are several different ways to measure income disparity (Galbraith, 2012). The most general way is to measure the disparity in household income. Household income includes not wage income but also dividend income and capital gains from investments such as stocks, bonds, or tangible assets. It includes the income of all of the individuals in the household, not just a single person. Including all sources of income in a household will show the largest income disparity because the wealthy tend to own more stocks, bonds, or tangible investments than median or low-income households. A second way to measure income disparity is to measure expenditures or spending. Spending should be closely related to income, however, the wealthy tend to spend a smaller percent of their income than median or low-income households. A third way to measure income disparity is to measure only wage income. Wage income is a more narrow measure of disparity since it does not include all sources of income but there is more data available to measure changes in inequality over time.

There are several different ways of mathematically displaying income disparity. Analysts can use many different factors to explore income inequality relationships such as by education levels (Yellen, Speech to the Center for the Study of Democracy, 2006). Figure 35 illustrates the rising income disparity using U.S. real income percentiles of men based on data from Table P54 – Total Money Income of People produced by the U.S. Census Bureau. In this analysis, a person in the 90th percentile is richer than a person in the 80th percentile. All of the real income levels have been normalized to 100% in 1980 and changes are expressed relative to the 80th percentile. This is why all of the lines intersect in the year 1980. Figure 35 does not suggest there was equality in 1980, but rather compares the inequality of 1980 to the inequality of later years.

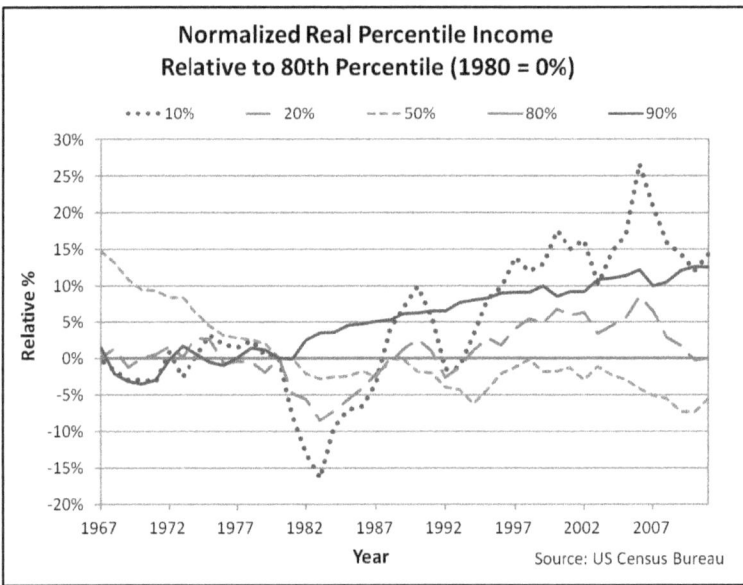

Figure 35 : Normalized U.S. Real Income Percentiles – Men

The 80th percentile was chosen as a reference point because this percentile best illustrates how the other percentiles are moving. Using the median percentile (50%) as a reference point would have just shown everyone gaining on the median. Figure 35 shows how the median percentile has been declining relative to the other percentiles. The 10th and 20th real income percentiles are the most volatile due to measurement error. Note that in terms of real income, the 10th percentile has kept up with the 90th percentile. Similarly, the 20th percentile has also kept up with the 80th percentile. This means, for example, that the real income ratio between the 90th and 10th percentiles has not changed significantly. The median real income percentile is the only percentile declining in Figure 35. This illustrates that it is the middle class that is taking the brunt of the decline in relative incomes.

There is a period from the 1996 to 2003 where the median real income level almost stopped declining relative to the 80th and 90th real income levels. Is the temporary spike in U.S. business investment that occurred during the technology bubble responsible for raising the real incomes of all percentiles?

Before discussing some of the potential sources of rising inequality, it is important to note that time series of inequality measurements like Figure 35 are not necessarily measuring the same people. These measurements are like snapshots of a system. It is measuring the state of the system but doesn't necessarily explain how the individuals are moving within the system due to opportunities or life cycle earnings.

A country that attracts uneducated, poor individuals to achieve a better life can have income disparity simply because new immigrants have arrived. To measure the success of an economic system and optimize its inequality, one must also study the income mobility of its population and to what extent the low-income individuals and their children are able to move up over time to become median and high-income individuals.

Examining top income percentiles, like the debate over the top 1% relies on IRS tax filing data. However, taxable income depends on the willingness to realize the income and pay the required taxes. Consequently, taxable income is a function of tax rates. With lower tax rates, individuals are more willing to realize income. The data shows that the share of income taken by the top 10% has risen from 35% in 1980 to 48% in 2011 (Saez, 2012). The share of income earned by the top 1% has almost doubled to 20%. Yet almost all of the increase happened before 2000. The reduction in U.S. tax rates from 1980 to 2000 coincides with the rising share of income for the top 1%. It is no coincidence that the share of income for the top percentiles has returned to the same levels that existed in the 1920s and 1930s (Piketty & Saez, 2003); before large federal income taxes were imposed on individuals and corporations began using perks to compensate highly valued employees to avoid excessive taxes.

There is rising income disparity in the U.S. coming at the expense of the middle class. However, it doesn't require misinterpreting data about this year's top 1% to document it.

A Global Phenomenon

The conventional market-based argument for changes in relative wages between segments of the economy is that the rising wage disparity is due to a skills gap. There is a mismatch between the demand for workers with certain skills and the supply of workers with those skills. When segmenting by education level, the claim is that workers with higher levels of education are able to obtain high-wage jobs while workers who do not finish high school must take low-wage jobs. While this skills gap may provide a reasonable explanation for the existence of wage inequality, it is on much weaker ground to claim the skills gap is also responsible for <u>changes</u> in wage inequality over time (Galbraith, 2012). Why would these skills be more valuable today than in 1980?

Another claim is that workers in high-growth industries obtain higher wages and are responsible for rising income disparity. It is easier for these advanced industries to compete on value while other low-skill industries have to compete on price (Galbraith, 2012). This explanation is also reasonable for the existence of wage inequality but why would the income disparity from today's growth industries be so different from the growth industries of 1980? Perhaps the pace of change from the information and medical technology revolution is playing a much greater role today? The machine freed man from the limits of his muscles and the computer is freeing man from the limits of his brain (Brynjolfsson & McAfee, 2012).

The evolution of jobs in the economy can also play a role in income disparity. Simon Kuznets proposed that changes in U.S. income disparity around 1955 were the result of workers moving from low-wage agriculture jobs to high-wage manufacturing jobs. He suggested an inverted U curve, like a sine wave, to model the transition and its effect on income disparity (Galbraith, 2012). The larger the wage differential, the greater the impact on inequality the migration will have.

Income disparity increased at the beginning of the transition as workers gradually migrated to high-wage manufacturing jobs, peaked in the middle of the transition, and decreased at the end of the transition as fewer workers were left in low-wage agricultural jobs.

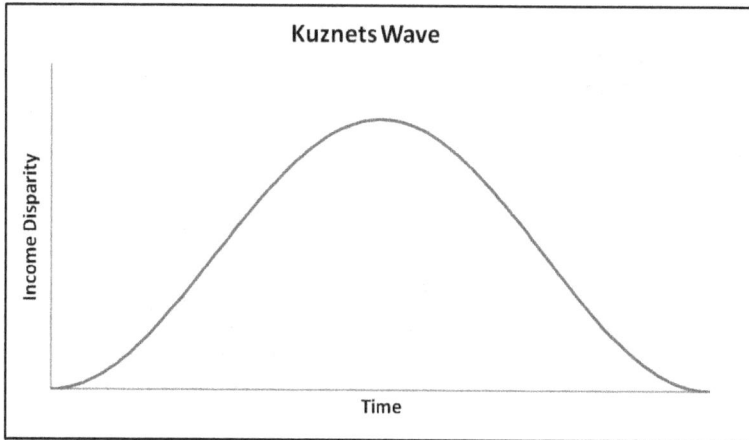

Figure 36: Kuznets Curve or Kuznets Wave

The Kuznets wave can similarly be applied to the migration from manufacturing jobs to service industry jobs in the developed economies. Manufacturing jobs have been declining globally for over 70 years due to increasing automation. In 1940, about 35% of employment was in the manufacturing sector. In 1980, it had declined to 20% of employment. In 2010 it represented less than 10% of total employment (Washington, 2010). The number of manufacturing jobs is even declining in China (Worstall, 2012). Could this transition of just 10% of the workforce to a service economy over the past 30 years explain some of the decline in median real wages for men relative to the 80th percentile from 1980? Perhaps a small portion if the wage differentials were large.

It seems that whatever is causing the rising inequality is a global phenomenon or globally coordinated. In a panel regression of inequality data to estimate the parameters of the Kuznets curve, the results show that starting in 1980, the global time-effect variables start to rise and accounts for essentially all of the increase in income disparity until 1998 when the analysis ends (Galbraith, 2012). A time-effect variable is added to allow for an explanation like "because it is 1992, 1993, 1994…". This is a very important clue to diagnosing the problem. The analysis demonstrated that almost all countries, including non-OECD countries, experienced basically the same phenomenon of rising income inequality over the same time period of 1980 to 1998.

Perhaps the education and employment of women is a global phenomenon not adequately represented. One recent study demonstrated that assortative mating could explain all of the increase in household income inequality in the U.S. between 1960 and 2005 (Jeremy

Greenwood, 2014). It wasn't because women were more likely to work or that they were earning more money that explained the rise in inequality. Instead, the rise in household income inequality was explained by the differences in marriage patterns from 1960 to 2005. Today, women are marrying men with income potentials similar to their own. This study does not imply that assortative mating is the sole reason for the rise in income inequality, just that it is a good candidate for a portion of the increase.

Demographic changes could also affect the percentile ratios over time. For example, the real income ratios between an upper and median percentile depends on age and peaks at around 50 years old for men (Auten, Gee, & Turner, 2013). Perhaps the influence of the Baby Boomers is also a small factor in the rise of U.S. income inequality.

Trade and Government-Created Profits

After taking into account demographic and cultural changes, any rise in income disparity should be due to a change in bargaining power between the percentiles.

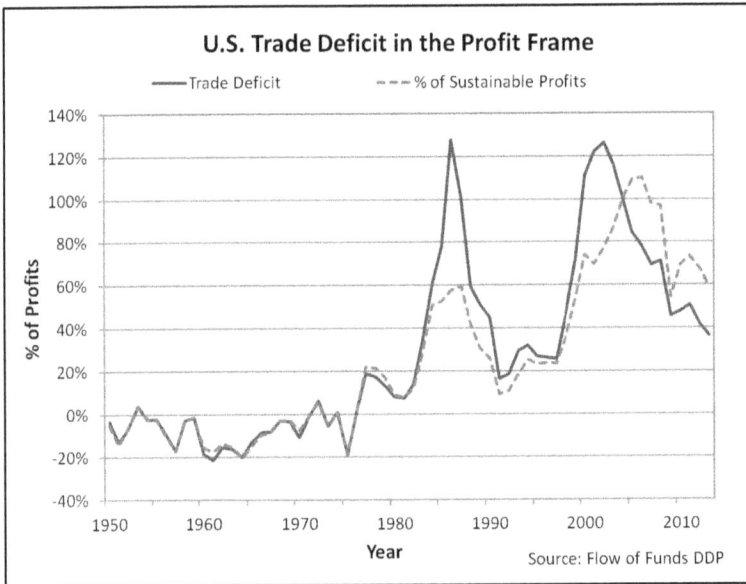

Figure 37: U.S. Trade Deficit as a Percent of Profits

Figure 37 illustrates the U.S. trade deficit as a percent of profits. If rising trade imbalances are responsible for a portion of the increase in income inequality, the imbalances and the government's desire to compensate for lost profits must change the bargaining power between the percentiles. This can be accomplished from the following policies,

- Forcing workers to compete on absolute wages rather than relative wages (see below).
- Creating excessive profits for both the surplus and deficit countries.
- Encouraging rising executive compensation.

The theory of trade is based on comparative advantage which says that trade is based on relative wage differences rather than absolute wage differences. However, this theory assumes balanced trade. When trade is not balanced, workers are forced to compete on absolute wages with foreign workers. Trade imbalances financed by foreign official reserves and the threat of outsourcing could explain the difficulty in the median income percentile maintaining its purchasing power compared to normalized wages bargained for under a more balanced-trade economic regime. Trade imbalances financed by foreign official reserves have the potential to change not only relative wages but the number of workers, as a percent of the labor force, subject to the threat of outsourcing. If governments returned to balanced trade, middle to low income percentiles would have more bargaining power relative to high-income percentiles.

The creation of profits by governments across the entire global economy may also be responsible for the global phenomenon of rising income disparity since 1980. For a country running a trade surplus like China, its government creates profits for their industries by setting their currency below fair value, generating export profits, demand for risk, and raising the value of their stock markets. On the other hand, countries like the U.S. have compensated for their trade deficit by increasing government deficits and guaranteeing mortgage debt to create profits. Both sides of the trade imbalance can see rising income disparity due to the government creation of profits that benefit the top percentiles relative to workers who are forced to compete on absolute wages. The current profit bubble due to quantitative easing is an example. The actions and reactions of governments could be responsible for a portion of the global phenomenon.

Finally, much has been written about rising executive compensation with stock options and a winner-take-all economy. Rising executive compensation can result from bargaining or taking advantage of a windfall. A windfall for executives could be either rising profits or Price/Earnings (P/E) multiples in the stock market. If profits are weak, executives cannot take an excessive share of profits for long. Similarly, if P/E ratios are low, executives cannot take an excessive share of stock outstanding for long.

Galbraith reveals a very strong relationship between the NASDAQ Composite Index with household income disparity from 1970 to 2004 due to the rising use of stock options and the ownership of stock by the wealthy (Galbraith, 2012). Once again, the NASDAQ Composite Index's dependence on profits and P/E multiplies leads us back to the source of profits in an economy.

Normally a rising stock market implies economic optimism and economic growth that benefits all income percentiles. However, when government policies are primarily responsible for creating profits, a rising stock market doesn't necessarily imply sustainable optimism or a fair allocation of bargaining power to all income percentiles.

In explaining the rise in the U.S. debt to GDP ratio, we examined how important home equity extraction was to the "credit supply", the growth of the mutual fund industry, and how rising household leverage created profits instead of business investment. The rise in government guaranteed mortgage debt as illustrated in Figure 20 of Chapter 5 also shows the same "takeoff" point around 1980 as the debt/GDP ratio and rising income disparity. Rather than pay down a mortgage with a low tax-deductible interest rate, U.S. households invested a larger share of their wealth in mutual funds. Demand for risk supported the stock market and provided a windfall for any executive with stock options.

The rise in income disparity from 1980 was accompanied by rising profits as a percent of GDP, falling interest rates, rising P/E ratios, larger business entities, and the creation of entirely new industries. All of these factors were windfalls and played a role in supporting executive compensation and bidding up the wages of certain skills or industries. A large portion of the rise in U.S. income disparity probably resulted from high-income earners taking advantage of the additional profits created by government budget deficits, housing policies, and quantitative easing.

It is also important to note that when the business sector doesn't have to create their share of profits for an economy and can rely on government deficits and housing "credit supply", then executive compensation is more easily justified. Businesses do not have to borrow money to invest in a project. Ample profits are available courtesy of these other sectors. There is less of a trade-off between investing in a necessary project and increasing executive compensation. While correlation does not imply causation, if the business sector had to create 60% of the profits in a balanced-trade economy, perhaps executive compensation would not be so easy to justify and income disparity might decline to a certain extent.

Taxing the Winners

Given the difficulty in determining the causes of rising income disparity, one political reaction is to raise taxes on the winners. As we discovered in the previous chapter, investments and taxes are substitutes. When you tax the rich, you are actually taxing what they were going to invest in. It is important that governments do not sabotage their economies like Mao, Pol Pot, or Lenin in the name of equality or pseudo equal opportunity.

The culture and mobility of labor may also decline if after-tax wages are forced to be too equal. This is dangerous because the work ethic changes from one of finding a job that has the highest value and might require more effort to finding a job that requires the least effort. The culture changes from giving to taking. This is why economies that demand equal outcomes fail. It is not just that the central planners can't process all of the price signals in an economy to make good planning decisions; it is also because their desire for equal outcomes transforms the culture from maximizing giving to maximizing taking.

Many of the analyses surrounding the cause of income inequality or the harm of income inequality rely on faulty statistical methods (Snowdon, 2011). The conclusions rely on outliers or they use selective data and omit explanatory factors. They look for unique features of a country and then intentionally use that kind of data in their analysis to skew results to their desired conclusion. They use correlation to imply causation. Think of any unique characteristic of the U.S. and you can use it statistically to show it is correlated with income inequality and then take the further step to declare it as a cause of income inequality or vice versa. Reducing social problems is not as simple as throwing money at the problem through redistribution; a proper diagnosis is required and the investments must be productive.

There is an optimal level of income disparity that should be targeted that provides opportunity for all with adequate rewards for effort and value. Because of the multitude of possible explanatory variables and the income mobility of workers, income disparity is very difficult to analyze and definitively understand. While not certain, the question is raised whether income disparity would decline if balanced trade was enforced and governments relied more on sustainable business investment for their primary source of profits rather than currency manipulation, government deficits, and excessive housing "credit supply" growth.

In this chapter we briefly examined the problem of rising income disparity in the U.S. since 1980. Perhaps cultural phenomena like changing demographics or assortative mating explain some of the increase in income inequality. In addition, the use of foreign official reserves to finance trade imbalances along with government deficits and home equity extraction to compensate may have played a supporting role in the global phenomenon of rising income disparity for both the lending countries and the borrowing countries. On the road to economic prosperity, governments should restore bargaining power by returning to balanced trade, create the conditions to maximize equal opportunity, and promote business investment as a source of profits.

Chapter 11 - Federal Reserve Policy

This chapter will examine the consequences of the dual mandate of the Federal Reserve, how to properly determine an inflation target, and to what extent inflation affects the growth rate of an economy.

The Dual Mandate

The U.S. Federal Reserve is subject to a dual mandate. The Full Employment and Balanced Growth Act of 1978 (Humphrey-Hawkins Act) mandates both price stability and full employment as the objectives of the Federal Reserve. This differs from the mandate of the European Central Bank which is just price stability (Hosli, 2005).

The dual mandate significantly diminishes the independence of the Federal Reserve. The independence of a central bank is only relevant during an economic crisis. When government policy is prudent, employment is usually strong and the Fed only needs to concentrate on price stability. It is in times of political dysfunction when the independence is needed but the full employment portion of the dual mandate prevents independence.

When Paul Volker raised the Fed Funds interest rate to its peak of 20% in June 1981, he was not confronting a government that was borrowing too much. Instead, he was confronting inflation expectations and the demands for accommodations from private interest groups. This allowed the Federal Reserve to pursue its dual mandate with the support of the government even though interest rates at 20% pushed the economy into a recession. The executive and legislative branches were not entirely at odds with Federal Reserve policy.

The situation the Federal Reserve faces today is a very different situation where the economy is being supported largely by U.S. federal budget deficits. To confront the government, if capital flight accelerates, would plunge the U.S. economy into a severe recession or depression and would be hard to justify under the dual mandate.

In 2012, the Federal Reserve embarked on a third quantitative easing policy that encompassed purchasing $85 Billion of Treasuries and mortgage-backed securities every month until the unemployment rate was reduced (Monetary Policy Releases, 2012). Without quantitative easing, U.S. households would have most likely had to finance the large government deficits during this time. If so, this would have lowered consumer spending and profits. However, rather than limit the purchases to $25 billion in line with previous levels of profit creation, the Fed generated a profit bubble hoping that this would put people back to work sooner and fulfill the employment mandate.

The Federal Reserve's quantitative easing policy would be fine if it wasn't creating another bubble and the U.S. federal government was taking advantage of the Fed's support and adopting prudent policies that transition the U.S. towards a more sustainable economy. Unfortunately, there is no evidence that the U.S. is transitioning to a more sustainable economy. Rather it looks as if the U.S. federal government is unwilling to make the tough decisions. At the end of 2012, the U.S. trade deficit continues to rise and it is unlikely that a sufficient level of tax reform will be enacted to convince businesses to invest in the U.S. It is possible that the U.S. has other global interests that it is balancing at the expense of business investment. Would balanced trade with China induce a financial crisis in China and lead to shortages of essential goods? Would balanced trade with Europe push the European Union over the edge? If so, it is the middle class that is paying the hefty premiums of this insurance policy.

A truly independent Federal Reserve would recognize the dangers of long-term financial repression, excessive debt to GDP, overvalued assets backing Federal Reserve Notes, and a lack of U.S. business investment. The Fed's unwillingness to criticize the government on several issues may mean they are not avoiding a crisis but rather just delaying a crisis. If the Federal Reserve waits until inflation exceeds its target or capital flight develops, it will not be able to meet either of its mandates.

A quantitative easing policy with a higher probability of meeting both mandates would threaten to withhold some support if the political stalemate was not broken and more prudent policies adopted. Setting a strict timeline for the end of quantitative easing or capping Federal Reserve assets as a percentage of GDP, rather than subjective criteria like the unemployment rate, would squarely put the responsibility on the executive and legislative branches of the government for any economic consequences. It looks like only economic pressure will force the federal government to acknowledge reality and make some difficult political decisions.

Without a transition to a more sustainable source of profits, the U.S. economy will eventually experience a decline in profits either from an end of quantitative easing or a political reaction to rising inflation or excessive government debt. Each year the federal government compensates for lost profits its debt burden grows and it becomes more vulnerable and weak. The Federal Reserve should try to administer a controlled dose of economic pressure by refraining from quantitative easing and targeting sustainable profits now rather than risk an overdose later. Continuous bailouts without government accountability will make it more difficult to find a political resolution and delay the additional U.S. business investment that is needed. Avoiding inflation as the tipping point is reached will be like running a gauntlet. Exit strategies tend to be very bumpy mountain passes with cliffs on both sides of the road.

Unfortunately, given the dual mandate and the inability to violate the law, the Federal Reserve can be expected to resort to quantitative easing at every sign of economic weakness. Rather than confronting foreign central bank financing of U.S. trade deficits, the Federal Reserve appears to have adopted a policy of competitive devaluation in what is essentially an inflation arms race, unlikely to generate additional U.S. business investment, and possibly leading to greater instability further down the road.

The Inflation Target

In recent years, the Federal Reserve has explored the possibility of setting an inflation target. In January of 2012, the Fed specified its "longer-run goal for inflation" at 2% per year (Longer-Run Goals and Policy Strategy, 2012). The Fed believes that by publicly setting this target, inflation expectations will be better anchored and it will be less likely that a group or coalition will demand an inflationary accommodation.

In a normal economy, some wages will fall relative to others. The Federal Reserve targets a little inflation to smooth the adjustment process. With a little inflation, the Federal Reserve believes there is less likely to be a confrontation or an escalation that would damage the entire economy with strikes and shortages.

To arrive at an inflation target, the Federal Reserve can monitor four input variables, 1) productivity, 2) bank credit growth or money supply growth, 3) household "credit supply" growth such as mortgage debt growth, and 4) some measure of growth in the labor force or total hours worked. With an estimate of productivity, labor force growth, and household "credit supply" growth, the Federal Reserve could target bank credit growth to achieve its inflation target. If bank credit growth is not adequate, the Federal Reserve could use quantitative easing to make up the difference as it did in 2012 while setting limits to insure its balance sheet does not exceed a certain percent of GDP.

Equation 13: Inflation Target

$$Inflation\ Target = + Money\ Supply\ Growth\ Rate$$
$$+ Credit\ Supply\ Growth\ Rate$$
$$- Productivity\ Growth\ Rate$$
$$- Labor\ Force\ Growth\ Rate$$

In this equation, the growth rate of the money supply and household "credit supply" should be subject to limits so that unsustainable levels of profits are not created. If the federal government ran a budget deficit that could breach the sustainable limit, the Treasury Department should be required to borrow the excess from the household sector so as not to create unsustainable profits.

While several factors affect the link between inflation and money supply growth, a steady state relationship should be assumed. If government debt is being used to support the non-working population, then balanced trade is the best way to support the working population and achieve the inflation target rather than a profit bubble financed by excessive lending or quantitative easing.

When productivity surges and profits have reached their sustainable limit, allowing inflation to fall below the inflation target is the best policy. Figure 38 illustrates the growth rate of productivity for the U.S. since 1950. A polynomial curve is also fitted to smooth the data.

When U.S. labor productivity was strong from 1996 to 2004, the Federal Reserve should have targeted a lower inflation rate even as low as 0%. By allowing household debt growth to get out of hand because productivity was strong and inflation was low, the Federal Reserve facilitated an eventual housing bubble that the U.S. economy is still dealing with several years later.

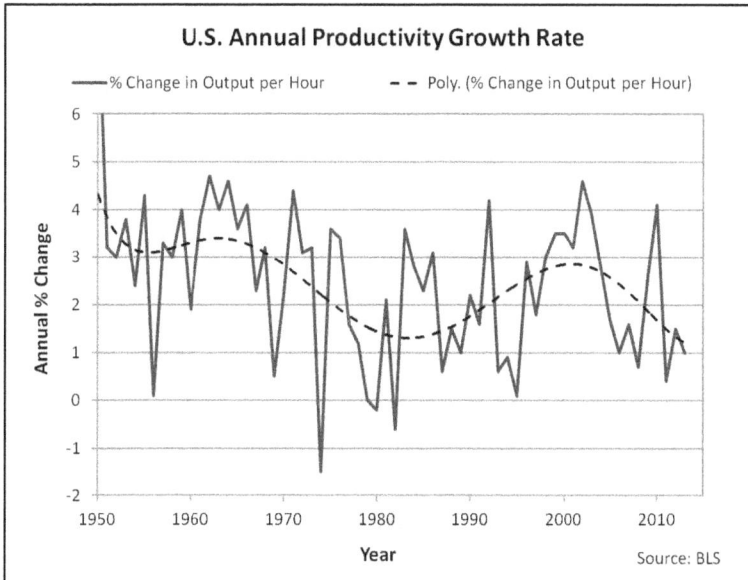

Figure 38: U.S. Measure of Productivity Growth Rate

Inflation vs. Growth

John Maynard Keynes wrote "Lenin said to have declared that the best way to destroy the capitalist system was to debauch the currency. By a continuing process of inflation governments can confiscate, secretly and unobserved, an important part of the wealth of their citizens. By this method they not only confiscate, but they confiscate arbitrarily; and, while the process impoverishes many, it actually enriches some. The sight of this arbitrary rearrangement of riches strikes not only at security, but at confidence in the equity of the existing distribution of wealth. Those to whom the system brings windfalls, beyond their deserts and even beyond their expectations or desires, become 'profiteers,' who are the object of the hatred of the bourgeoisie, whom the inflationism has impoverished, not less than of the proletariat. As the inflation proceeds and the real value of the currency fluctuates wildly from month to month, all permanent relations between debtors and creditors, which form the ultimate foundation of capitalism, become so utterly disordered as to be almost meaningless; and the process of wealth-getting degenerates into a gamble and a lottery. Lenin was certainly right. There is no subtler, no surer means of overturning the existing basis of society than to debauch the currency. The process engages all the hidden forces of economic law on the side of destruction, and does it in a manner which not one man in a million is able to diagnose." (Keynes, 1919)

It is not controversial that hyperinflation destroys countries, but what about just a medium amount of inflation? During difficult times, advocates of growth will suggest more inflation to reduce the unemployment rate. The relationship between inflation and growth has been investigated by many economists. However, with an understanding of inflation as due to either a shortage or an accommodation, the relationship to growth is not difficult to predict. Investigating the growth rates across different countries and eliminating outliers and periods of hyperinflation, the data produces a result as one would expect. Real growth slows in the period of rising inflation and then accelerates after the period of inflation ends. There does not appear to be a relationship between the long-run growth rate and inflation (Motley, 1998).

Because inflation is a tax, it is not surprising that it would slow real growth in the short-run. If the inflation is caused by a supply shortage, the shortage constrains growth. If the inflation is due to an accommodation, it is probably due to an unwillingness to address structural issues that are limiting growth and productivity. Until the shortage is resolved or the structural issues addressed, growth slows. Once resolved, however, the economy enters a period of catch-up with strong growth. Investments that were delayed during rising inflation are initiated as stability and optimism returns. The net effect is that inflation slows or delays the rise in a country's standard of living. Eventually a country catches up but its prosperity is delayed. If the goal of a government is to raise the standard of living for its citizens, then it is wise to keep inflation contained.

As the European Central Bank has discovered in the European Crisis, without pressure, politicians will not make the difficult choices. Advocates of growth will occasionally propose inflation as a way to break a political stalemate between interest groups. If the stalemate involves taxes, inflation acts like a wealth tax that can circumvent the stalemate. With the U.S. running large budget deficits and unwilling to adopt policies to promote adequate U.S. business investment, the U.S. could gradually see rising inflation if capital flight ignites. If inflation expectations rise above inflation targets, this may slow real growth and postpone standard of living gains.

The Economic Lighthouses

Over the next several years, the Federal Reserve will have to walk a tightrope to guide the creation of profits without creating more bubbles or entering a depression.

The economic lighthouses that the Federal Reserve will need on the road to prosperity include 1) the amount of profits created in the economy, 2) the source of profits and their dependence on housing, government, and business, and 3) the purchase of government securities by banks or households if pressure needs to be put on the federal government.

The Federal Reserve should be pushing harder for balanced trade and policies that promote business investment rather than trying to look apolitical. If the federal government refuses to deal with the difficult policy decisions that the road to economic prosperity requires, the Federal Reserve may have to put some stress on the economy to motivate the politicians.

The Federal Reserve should allow long-term interest rates to gradually rise until either banks or the household sector are willing to purchase Treasury securities. The rise in rates or the reduction in profits might be enough to pressure the federal government to adopt the correct policies that generate U.S. business investment. This would also allow the Federal Reserve to exit its quantitative easing programs.

The dual mandate makes it unlikely that the Federal Reserve would put stress on the government when only the government deficits are supporting the economy and keeping it out of a depression. More likely, the Fed will attempt to print money upon any sign of economic weakness as a way to strengthen employment and regain competitiveness but will be countered with competitive devaluations from other countries.

In this chapter, we examined the dual mandate of the Federal Reserve and how unlikely it is that the Fed will violate the law and confront the U.S. federal government to force policy changes in order to balance trade and generate additional business investment in the U.S. We also discussed how a small inflation target is probably optimal and why inflation below the target is acceptable in periods of strong productivity in order to avoid unsustainable debt growth. The Federal Reserve will have to walk a tightrope over the next several years in order to avoid more bubbles or an outright economic depression.

Chapter 12 - Stages of a Nation's Bankruptcy

There are usually three stages to a nation's bankruptcy that one can use to assess the dysfunction and desperation of a government. The first stage involves bank failures, the second stage adds excessive government debt-to-GDP ratios, and the third stage adds raiding the pension assets of the country. By the end of the third stage, the wealth and security of the nation has typically been squandered and default or inflation is unavoidable.

Stage 1 – Bank Failures

Banks are a political entity as well as a business entity. They are a political entity because their lending is regulated and their existence is at the discretion of the government. If a government doesn't like what banks are doing, governments will create banks to do the government's bidding. This is why the first stage of a nation's bankruptcy usually involves bank failures.

Banks are like off-balance-sheet entities of governments. If a government doesn't want to directly borrow money to invest in a project, it can use banks to borrow or create the money to make the investment. Because banks are beholden to the government, they tend to assist the government in their endeavors. It is off-balance-sheet because the assets and liabilities of the banks do not show up on the balance sheet of the government. Using banks to do their bidding makes governments look healthier than they may be.

In some cases, the banks are reluctant to take excessive risk. In these cases, the government will usually create banking entities to circumvent the banks. Andrew Jackson witnessed the damage these government banks did in Kentucky and Tennessee and this influenced his decision to shut down the government-chartered Second Bank of USA.

Today, Fannie Mae and Freddie Mac are essentially government-chartered banks that were created because the government was not happy with the amount of risk that private banks were taking in home lending. In order to essentially take over a large portion of mortgage lending, the government created these two entities with government guarantees. In 2012, along with the government-owned entity Ginnie Mae, the government guaranteed close to 90% of all mortgages underwritten (Min, 2012). Student loan guarantees and subsidies are another example of how government creates its own bank or guarantees when it is not happy with the amount of risk that private banks are taking or its cost. On a grander scale, quantitative easing forcibly injects bank deposits into the banking system to induce risk taking and inflation.

The financial crisis of 2008 had many causes. While there were many ways that the financial crisis could have been prevented, there was only one way it could have been created to the extent it was. The banks, mortgage brokers, appraisers, real estate agents, rating agencies, investors, and individual borrowers all could have prevented the excesses from developing. *But only the government guarantees on any outcome could have created the size of the mortgage excesses in the first place. Everyone was taking advantage of the government guarantee.*

The close links between the German banks and the German government also played a role in the European crisis. German banks lent to profligate Southern European countries in a version of vendor financing to support the German economy. Vendor financing is when a company selling a product lends the buyer the money. It is like giving the product away and hoping to get paid back later if the buyer is successful. Vendor financing can easily be abused if the buyer lacks the ability to pay. As witnessed in the technology bubble, giving equipment to insolvent start-ups who have no way of paying for the equipment looks more like channel stuffing to pump up revenues or profits and eventually leads to write-offs and losses.

Stage 2 - Government Debt-to-GDP

Once the financial sector's capital is squandered and needs a bailout, the government usually bails out the banks. This is because credit is like blood flowing through the veins of the economy. If bank credit and the money multiplier effect are shut down, this major network hub that assists in creating profits in an economy shrinks and the country plunges into depression and deflation.

The misallocation of capital that causes the financial crisis usually requires structural reforms to transition to sustainable growth. If the government is not willing to adopt the structural reforms, the government will take the place of the banks in misallocating capital and begin to accrue deficit spending.

Eventually, the government's debt-to-GDP ratio approaches unsustainable levels and it begins to face difficulties financing its budget deficit. This usually requires the government to choose between 1) adopting structural reforms, 2) monetizing debt to delay the eventual default leading to inflation, or 3) the third stage of bankruptcy.

Stage 3 – Raiding the Pensions

In the final stage of a nation's bankruptcy, the country raids the government pension fund to postpone the day of reckoning. If the pension fund can only own the same government's securities, like the Social Security Trust Fund, then this stage is irrelevant because the government has already taken control of the assets.

One way to raid the pension fund is by reducing the contribution rate. By simply not funding the pension, the cash flows of the government appear better than they are. Another way is by forcing the pension funds to buy the government's debt and thus finance the government.

Argentina

While the three stages of bankruptcy are typically the domestic path to default or excessive inflation, Argentina illustrates the bankruptcy process under a "gold-standard" that takes advantage of domestic and foreign investors before defaulting. Southern European countries in the Euro are on a similar path except the Northern European countries keep lending money.

In 1991, Argentina was in a period of hyperinflation due to government fiscal and monetary excess with inflation at 84% per year (Viable Opposition, 2011). As the inflation wreaked havoc on the economy, the government with the help and advice of the International Monetary Fund (IMF) decided to alter course and introduced the "Convertibility Plan" to fix the foreign exchange rate of the peso to one U.S. dollar (Hornbeck, 2010). Thus, the peso was "dollarized". Every peso would be backed by a U.S. dollar. Instead of using gold reserves to back the peso, Argentina used U.S. dollar reserves.

For a few years, the economy grew and inflation was low, but the government's desire to subsidize and spend more money than it received in taxes hadn't changed. The government decided that since it couldn't print pesos, it would just borrow U.S. dollars. The U.S. dollar proceeds of the debt were converted to pesos and squandered domestically.

If a country on the gold standard sells their gold, the amount of currency in the system must decrease and causes deflation. When the Argentina government borrowed U.S. dollars, it was equivalent to promising to sell gold had they been on the gold standard. Their U.S. dollar debt represented a promise to sell the U.S. dollars reserves later. When their U.S. dollar government debt was netted with their currency reserves, there were fewer net reserves remaining. Argentine government's desire to spend more than they received in taxes was leading them down a catastrophic road to deflation.

The Convertibility Plan also failed because they linked the peso to the U.S. dollar. They linked the peso to a currency that is the target of currency manipulation for practically the entire world. After a few years, Argentina's neighbors had devalued their currencies relative to the U.S. dollar so that Argentina was no longer competitive. Not only was the government borrowing money but the country was now running large trade deficits. The trade deficits also acted like reducing the amount of reserves backing their currency as well as taking profits from the economy. Capital flight eventually took hold as investors tried to get their money out of the country (Viable Opposition, 2011).

In 2001, the scheme collapsed and Argentina defaulted on $100 Billion in debt (Sturzenegger & Zettelmeyer, 2006). Argentina blamed the IMF and could rightly argue that they were victims of currency manipulation, although their own policies were the primary cause (Wijnholds, 2011). Had they not permitted the government borrowing, their economy would have suffered at the hands of the currency manipulators. Just like the U.S. tries to counter the effects of a trade deficit, Argentina tried to counter the effects; but without a central bank like the Federal Reserve to monetize their debt with quantitative easing programs.

Argentina follows a socialist economic model like Venezuela with large subsidies. With their new currency, they have imposed capital controls to prevent their citizens from buying foreign currency (Newbery, 2011). They have nationalized private pension funds and transferred their assets to the government pension fund (Barrionuevo, 2008). In

2012 they nationalized majority ownership of YPF, the largest oil company in Argentina, because the company did not want to invest in Argentina (Romero & Minder, 2012). Without these measures, Argentina would be facing an investment boycott, capital flight, and hyperinflation that Germany experienced in the 1920s. When the business sector doesn't want to invest in a country, it's a sign that the government needs to reflect on its policies.

In 2012, Argentina now uses official foreign reserves to manipulate and devalue their currency like the rest of the world. They have approximately $50 Billion in reserves (Hornbeck, 2010). By manipulating their currency and having capital controls, the main issue for the government is to control inflation. Inflation is estimated to be between 10% and 20% and the government has taken over the statistics department (Rastello & Raszewski, 2012). With Argentina considered to be still in default internationally and with their excessive subsidies, they appear to be back on the conventional three-stage, domestic path to default and possibly returning to the inflation level of the 1980s.

Economics is like statistics. At an individual level, economic events are random. However, after millions of samples it stops being just random numbers and starts becoming mathematical functions. While governments can use banks, budget deficits, and pensions to delay paying the bill, eventually the bill must be paid.

Chapter 13 - The Political Road

This chapter examines some of the political obstacles the U.S. must overcome to begin its journey on the road to economic prosperity. It will require reflection as well as courage and perspective. The global economy really isn't that old. We are living through the growing pains of a global adolescence. The next century can be truly remarkable and with balanced trade and business investment the world can experience strong increases in standards of living.

To achieve global cooperation will require global leadership. With the U.S. position in the world today and the importance of the U.S. economy, there is an opportunity for U.S. leadership to bring about balanced trade without punishing trade.

Halfway There

The financial crisis of 2008 exposed the danger of using excessive amounts of leverage in housing to compensate for lost profits and a lack of business investment. Before the financial crisis, the U.S. trade deficit represented 6% of GDP. During the crisis, the U.S. trade deficit plunged to 2.5% of GDP. However, in 2012 the U.S. trade deficit has rebounded to 4% of GDP and business investment is still not producing its proper share of profit creation.

The financial crisis brought the U.S. almost halfway to a balanced trade economy as illustrated in Figure 39. Progress has been made even with the recent reversals. However, since the crisis, the U.S. has failed to adequately address the issue and introduce policies that will move the global economy the rest of the way towards balanced trade. Politicians are unwilling to take their place in history.

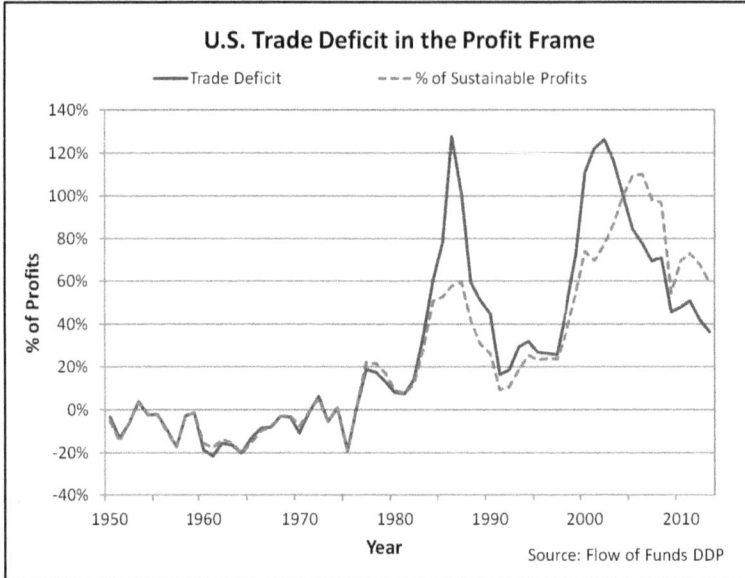

Figure 39: U.S. Trade Deficit as a Percent of Profits

The U.S. has been running large budget deficits as its main source of profits and the Federal Reserve has been monetizing most of it to avoid a depression. It is time to solve the problem. The motivation for this book was to use the profit frame to provide a different perspective so that the sources of the problem could be more clearly identified. By understanding the problem, the global economic community can start discussing solutions rather than treating symptoms. As Benjamin Franklin once said, "An ounce of prevention is worth a pound of cure".

The Difference between the Truth and Debating

Since 2004, the U.S. has been arguing about whether they should be in the right lane or the left lane when they go over the cliff. Both Democrats and Republicans have blamed people. The Democrats blame "the 1%" and the Republicans blame "the 47%".

There is a difference between debating and searching for the truth. Debating is just lobbing facts out to the public without regard for importance or context. Debating is a tit-for-tat event. Most people are tired of the spin. They want politicians who will respect them, stop debating, work with them on solutions, and tell them the truth. In 2008, President Obama talked about post-partisan politics. It was a powerful message that was not fulfilled. In 2012, he talked about one America.

To have one America, the political leaders of the U.S. will need to stop debating and seek the truth.

A favorite quote by Socrates is *"Strong minds discuss ideas, average minds discuss events, and weak minds discuss people."* The political leaders of the U.S. need to stop talking about people and start talking about solutions. The Republicans must respect the 47% who are looking for a solution and would benefit the most from balanced trade and a return of U.S. business investment. The 99% must respect the 1% as they are investing in people and ideas to make the world a better place.

The press is an institution of a country. A country with a strong journalistic ethic will more likely have a strong country. A free press is supposed to protect its citizens from the abuse of government and also hold the government accountable. The press can play a helpful role in promoting balanced trade and encouraging governments to adopt policies that will restore business investment to its proper level and avoid profit bubbles along the way. The U.S. needs to replace its one-legged stool, government as the main source of profit creation, with a three-legged stool. Each leg of the stool, government, business, and the household sector should create their proper sustainable share of profits without having it taken away by trade deficits. The press will be needed to achieve this goal.

Delaying Turmoil vs. Avoiding Turmoil

As of 2013, the path of least political resistance in the U.S. appears to be on a road heading towards more bubbles, collapses, and potentially severe partisanship without reform. To meaningfully deal with the future, the U.S. needs to not just delay turmoil but avoid turmoil. If the U.S. kicks the can down the road, putting forth half-measures, the middle class may pay an even larger price than they have already paid.

Politics is like a circle. There is a left side and a right side that reflects liberalism and conservatism, respectively. There is also a top half and bottom half that reflects freedom and authoritarianism, respectively. The U.S. was originally founded as an experiment somewhere near the top of the political circle. It is important that the U.S. stays in the upper half of the circle. With the U.S. government recently creating all of the profits, guaranteeing virtually all of the mortgages, and forcibly creating bank deposits, warning signs should be flashing. Quantitative easing to compensate for a lack of political courage only delays the eventual economic turmoil.

The Federal Reserve can play in important role in bringing the political parties to the table by being more transparent about the consequences of inaction. They should state upfront the future Fed policy that will confront the government when they assert their independence. They should criticize the growth in official foreign reserves. The Federal Reserve should set a transparent timeline or a cap on their assets as a percent of GDP. Then, not only the financial community but the politicians as well would see a transparent Federal Reserve policy. *If the Fed cares about transparency, make it transparent to the politicians.*

Successful Negotiating

The best negotiators are the people who ask the most questions and do the most research to understand what both sides want and are willing to accept. They acquire knowledge of the situation so that the best feasible solution can be obtained during the negotiation process (The Essentials of Negotiation, 2005). A negotiation is not just stating your demands; it also involves understanding why you and your opponent are making these demands.

The story of the two children fighting over an orange illustrates this vividly. One day a mother comes into the kitchen as her two boys are fighting over whom should get the last orange in the fruit bowl. As both boys implore her that it is he who should get the orange, she decides to do what is fair and cuts the orange in half and gives each boy one of the halves. The two boys then peel their halves of the orange. The older boy throws away the peelings and runs off with his half of the orange. The younger boy throws away the orange and keeps his half of the peelings. Had both boys asked why the other wanted the orange, they could have had a better solution than the one the mother dispensed with. Asking questions and understanding the situation are very important to obtain the best possible solution to a problem.

On the road to economic prosperity, it is important to understand when a particular opinion applies to an economic situation and when it does not. The economy is like a car with many potentially defective parts. It is important to diagnose the problem before suggesting how to fix it and demanding resources.

Education

Finally, the profit equation and the sources of profits should be taught as part of an economic curriculum. Graduates of business and economics should be able to answer the question "Where do profits come from?" The government should produce quarterly summaries of the economy's source of profits so that investors, journalists, educators, and thought leaders can identify bubbles and diagnose policy failures. Had this knowledge been disseminated and better understood from 1997 to 2007, perhaps Fannie Mae and Freddie Mac would not have been allowed to excessively guarantee mortgages, interest rates would not have been held so low, and the trade imbalances would have been addressed.

The "credit supply" should also be taught alongside the money supply. Foreign central bank reserves obtained from financing trade deficits inflict significant damage on economic equilibrium. The importance of the "shadow banking system", where securitized mortgage assets and bank deposit liabilities are converted into mutual fund assets and mutual fund holdings, respectively, should also be taught. Both the credit supply and the money supply affect the creation of debt growth, profits, economic growth, and prosperity.

Taxes

If you want to raise taxes, start by raising them on the portion of official foreign reserves that finance trade deficits.

Chapter 14 - The Road to Economic Prosperity

Profits come largely from debt growth used to purchase products included in an economy's GDP with the help of the banking system's money multiplier effect, dividend recycling, and vendor financing. By monitoring the source of profits, economists can identify bubbles and diagnose policy failures. The profit frame can provide a broader perspective and a better diagnosis of economic problems and potential solutions. By understanding where profits come from, the global economy can more easily identify the adjustments required so that the next century can be the greatest century.

The road to economic prosperity starts with moving towards a balanced trade economic regime. This may require taxing the portion of official foreign reserves that finance trade deficits to induce all countries to trade fairly. With balanced trade and a more competitive tax structure, business investment can return to the U.S. and replace the government deficits that have been propping up the U.S. economy.

If the federal government makes the correct policy choices, the Federal Reserve can return to a more normal monetary policy, refrain from further quantitative easing, and gradually remove the excess reserves from the banking system. Under a normal monetary policy with business investment creating its share of profits, the risks of confronting inflationary demands are reduced and the Fed can focus on its dual mandate.

By understanding where profits come from, thoughtful leaders can understand what policies are needed to generate sustainable growth and start educating people about the solutions rather than blaming others for the problem. The future holds great promise if the global community is willing to make the right decisions that lead us all down the road to economic prosperity.

BIBLIOGRAPHY

Adrian, T., Begalle, B., Copeland, A., & Martin, A. (2011, 12). Repo and Securities Lending. *Federal Reserve Bank of New York Staff Reports* .

Aizenman, J., & Lee, J. (2005). *International Reserves: Precautionary vs. Mercantilist Views, Theory and Evidence.* IMF Working Paper.

Assets and Liabilities of Commercial Banks in the United States . (2012, November). Retrieved November 2012, from Board of Governors of the Federal Reserve System: http://www.federalreserve.gov/releases/h8/about.htm

Auten, G., Gee, G., & Turner, N. (2013). Income Inequality, Mobility and Turnover at the Top in the U.S. 1987-2010. *American Economic Association.*

Back, A. (2011, April 18). Beijing Seeks to Cool Prices by Reining in Bank Lending. *The Wall Street Journal* .

Bank of Japan. (2003, December 26). Retrieved from Bank of Japan: http://www.boj.or.jp/en/announcements/release_2003/un0312a.htm/

Barrionuevo, A. (2008, October 21). Argentina Nationalizes $30 Billion in Private Pensions. *The New York Times* .

Bennett, M. J. (1996). *When Dreams Came True: The Gi Bill and the Making of Modern America* . Brassey's Inc.

Bernanke, B. S. (2002). On Milton Friedman's Ninetieth Birthday. *Conference to Honor Milton Friedman.* Chicago, Illinois.

Bernanke, B. S. (2009, January 13). *The Crisis and the Policy Response.* Retrieved 4 12, 2013, from Board of Governors of the Federal Reserve System: http://www.federalreserve.gov/newsevents/speech/bernanke200901 13a.htm

Bernanke, B. S. (2005). *The Global Saving Glut and the U.S. Current Account Deficit.* Retrieved from Federal Reserve: http://www.federalreserve.gov/boarddocs/speeches/2005/20050310 2/

Bernstein, J., & Mishel, L. (2007). Economy's Gains Fail To Reach Most Workers' Paychecks. *EPI Breifing Paper.* Economic Policy Institute.

BLS. (2012). *Hedonic Quality Adjustment in the CPI.* Retrieved November 24, 2012, from Bureau of Labor Statistics: http://www.bls.gov/cpi/cpihqaitem.htm

Board of Governers of the Federal Reserve System. (2005). *The Federal Reserve System : Purposes & Functions.* Washington, DC: Publication Committee : Federal Reserve System.

Boettke, P. J., & Smith, D. J. (2012). A Century of Accommodation: The Failed Record of Federal Reserve Independence. *GMU Working Paper in Economics* , No. 12-40.

Brock, H. W. (2012). *American Gridlock.* Hoboken, NJ: John Wiley & Sons, Inc.

Brynjolfsson, E., & McAfee, A. (2012). *Race Against the Machine: How the Digital Revolution is Acceslerating Innovation, Driving Productivty, and Irreversibly Transforming Employment and the Economy.* Digital Frontier Press.

Burghardt, G. (2003). *The Eurodollar Futures and Options Handbook.* New York: McGraw-Hill.

Campbell, A., LaBrosse, J. R., Mayes, D. G., & Singh, D. (2007). *Deposit Insurance.* New York: Palgrave Macmillan.

Caouette, J. B., Altman, E. I., Narayanan, P., & Nimmo, R. (2008). *Managing Credit Risk.* Hoboken, NJ: John Wiley & Sons, Inc.

Carnegie, A. (1889). Wealth. *North American Review* , 653-665.

(2011). *CBO 2011 Long-Term Budget Outlook.*

CBS News. (2009, February 11). *Greenspan Defends Low Interest Rates.* Retrieved from CBS News 60 Minutes: http://www.cbsnews.com/8301-18560_162-3257567.html

da Cost, P., & Alister, B. (2012, 9 13). Fed bets big in new push to rescue economy. *Reuters* .

Dalio, R. (20012). *How the Economic Machine Works.* Retrieved 2013, from http://www.bwater.com: http://www.bwater.com/Uploads/FileManager/research/how-the-economic-machine-works/How-the-Economic-Machine%20Works--A-Template-for-Understanding-What-is-Happening-Now-Ray-Dalio-Bridgewater.pdf

Das, S. (2014, April 16). *China's Shadow Banking System.* Retrieved 2014, from Economonitor.com: http://www.economonitor.com/blog/2014/04/chinas-shadow-banking-system/

Debt to the Penny. (2012, November). Retrieved November 2012, from Treasury Direct: http://www.treasurydirect.gov/NP/BPDLogin?application=np

Developing the Domestic Government Debt Market. (2007). Washington, D.C.: IBRD / The World Bank.

Diewert, W. E., Greenlees, J., & Hulten, C. R. (2010). *Price Index Concepts and Measurement* . Chicago, IL: University Of Chicago Press.

Dominguez, K. M. (n.d.). Retrieved from Princeton University Press: http://press.princeton.edu/chapters/reinert/4article_dominguez_steri lization.pdf

Drucker, P. F. (1993). *Post-Capitalist Society.* New York, NY: Harper Business.

ECB. (2013). *Bank Lending Survey* .

ECB. (2009). Financial Development in Emerging Economies - Stock-Taking and Policy Implications. *ECB Monthly Bulletin* .

ECB. (2014). *Why has the ECB introduced a negative interest rate?* Retrieved 2014, from http://www.ecb.europa.eu: http://www.ecb.europa.eu/home/html/faqinterestrates.en.html

Ehrenberg, R. (n.d.). *Tuition Rising: Why College Costs so Much.* Retrieved November 24, 2012, from Educause: http://net.educause.edu/ir/library/pdf/ffp0005s.pdf

Ewing, J. (2011, November 22). Europe's Banks Relying on Money From E.C.B. *The New York Times* .

Fair Tax. (2012, November 24). Retrieved November 24, 2012, from Wikipedia: http://en.wikipedia.org/wiki/FairTax

FDIC - Financial Institution Letters. (2008). Retrieved from FDIC: http://www.fdic.gov/news/news/financial/2008/fil08139.html

Federal Reserve Statistical Release. (2011). *Flow of Funds Accounts of the United States.* Washington, DC: Board of Governors of the Federal Reserve System.

Federal Reserve Statistical Releases. (2005). *The Flow of Funds Accounts of the United States.* Washington, DC: Board of Governors of the Federal Reserve System.

Feenstra, R. C., & Taylor, A. M. (2008). *International Economics.* New York, NY: Worth Publishers.

Fergusson, A. (2010). *When Money Dies.* New York: Public Affairs.

Fleischer, V. (2008, November 17). *Should We Tax Sovereign Wealth Funds.* Retrieved from The Yale Law Journal: http://yalelawjournal.org/the-yale-law-journal-pocket-part/scholarship/should-we-tax-sovereign-wealth-funds?/

Frank, R. H. (2010, October 16). *Income Inequality: Too Big to Ignore.* Retrieved November 24, 2012, from The New York Times: http://www.nytimes.com/2010/10/17/business/17view.html?_r=0

Freudenheim, M., & Williams Walsh, M. (2005, December 11). The Next Retirement Time Bomb. *The New York Times* .

Friedman, J., & Kraus, W. (2011). *Engineering the Financial Crisis : Systemic Risk and the Failure of Regulation.* Philadelphia, PA: University of Pennsylvania Press.

Friedman, M. (1970). *The Counter-Revolution in Monetary Theory.* Transatlantic Arts.

Friedman, M., & Schwartz, A. J. (1963). *A Monetary History of the United States, 1867-1960.* USA: Princeton University Press.

Galbraith, J. K. (2012). *Inequality and Instability.* New York: Oxford University Press.

Gale, W., Burman, L., & Suarez, R. (2005, March 3). *The Pros and Cons of a Consumption Tax.* Retrieved Novmeber 24, 2012, from Brookings Institute: http://www.brookings.edu/research/interviews/2005/03/03taxes-gale

Girotto, & Velloza. (2012, June 28). *Brazil's foreign exchange transaction tax in context.* Retrieved November 24, 2012, from IFLR: http://www.iflr.com/Article/3053395/Brazils-foreign-exchange-transaction-tax-in-context.html

Gordon, R. J. (2011). *Macroeconomics: Theory and Policy, 12th.* Prentice Hall.

Harvey, J. T. (2011, 5 30). What Actually Causes Inflation (and who gains from it). *Forbes* .

Henkels, S. V. (1928). *Andrew Jackson and the Bank of the United States: An interesting bit of history concerning "Old Hickory".*

Higher Education Price Index. (2012). Retrieved November 24, 2012, from Commonfund: http://www.commonfund.org/CommonfundInstitute/HEPI/Pages/default.aspx

Historical Income Tables. (2012, 11 13). Retrieved 11 13, 2012, from U.S. Census Bureau: http://www.census.gov/hhes/www/income/data/historical/people/

History of the Government Sponsored Enterprises. (2012). Retrieved from Federal Housing Finance Agency: http://www.fhfaoig.gov/LearnMore/History

Hornbeck, J. (2010). *Argentina's Defaulted Sovereign Debt: Dealing with the "Holdouts".* Congressional Research Service.

Hosli, M. O. (2005). *The Euro.* Boulder, CO: Lynne Rienner Publishers, Inc.

Huntsman, J. (2011). *Jon Huntsman on China.* Retrieved from The Political Guide: http://www.thepoliticalguide.com/Profiles/Governor/Utah/Jon_Huntsman/Views/China/

IS/LM Model. (2012, November 14). Retrieved November 14, 2012, from Wikipedia: http://en.wikipedia.org/wiki/IS/LM_model

Jaschik, S. (2008, March 12). *The Shrinking Professoriate*. Retrieved November 24, 2012, from Inside Higher Ed: http://www.insidehighered.com/news/2008/03/12/jobs

Jeremy Greenwood, N. G. (2014). Marry Your Like: Assortative Mating and Income Inequality. *American Economic Review, American Economic Association, vol. 104(5)* , 348-53.

Jolly, D. (2011, September 6). Swiss Central Bank Acts to Put a Cap on Franc's Rise. *The New York Times* .

Kalecki, M. (1972). *Essays in the Theory of Economic Fluctuations.* New York: Russell & Russell.

Kalecki, M. (1971). *Selected essays on the dynamics of the capitalist economy.* Cambridge University Press.

Kamin, S. B., Marazzi, M., & Schindler, J. W. (2004). Is China "Exporting Deflation"? *International Finance Discussion Papers* .

Keynes, J. M. (1919). The Economic Consequences of the Peace. PBS.org - Keynes on Inflation.

Klein, J. I. (2008). *Antitrust Enforcement and the Consumer.* Retrieved from Department of Justice: http://corporate.findlaw.com/litigation-disputes/antitrust-enforcement-and-the-consumer.html

Kobor, A. (2005). *What Determines U.S. Swap Spreads.* Washington, D.C.: World Bank Publications .

Koehler, D. M. (2000). *The Insider's Guide to Small Business Loans.* Central Point, OR: The Oasis Press / PSI Research.

Kroszner, R. S., & Melick, W. (2009). The Response of the Federal Reserve to the Recent Banking and Financial Crisis. *An Ocean Apart? Comparing Transatlantic Responses to the Financial Crisis.* Rome, Italy.

Krugman, P. (2010, 8 2). Why is Deflation Bad? *The New York Times* .

Levitt, S. D., & Dubner, S. J. (2005). *Freakonomics: A Rogue Economist Explores the Hidden Side of Everything.* New York: William Morrow Paperbacks.

Li, H. (2011, 3 2). Bill Gross: who will buy Treasuries when QE2 stops. *International Business Times* .

Longer-Run Goals and Policy Strategy. (2012, January 25). Retrieved November 24, 2012, from Board of Governors of the Federal Reserve System: http://www.federalreserve.gov/newsevents/press/monetary/20120125c.htm

Marginal Utility. (2012, November 14). Retrieved November 14, 2012, from Wikipedia: http://en.wikipedia.org/wiki/Marginal_utility

Min, D. (2012, May). *The Global Importance of Government Guarantees in Mortgage Finance.* Retrieved November 24, 2012, from Center for American Progress: http://www.americanprogress.org/wp-content/uploads/issues/2012/05/pdf/global_mortgages.pdf

Mitchell, J. (2012, June 10). New Course in College Costs. *The Wall Street Journal* .

Monetary Policy IOR FAQ. (2012). Retrieved from Federal Reserve: http://www.federalreserve.gov/monetarypolicy/ior_faqs.htm#1

Monetary Policy Releases. (2012, October 24). Retrieved November 24, 2012, from Board of Governors of the Federal Reserve System: http://www.federalreserve.gov/newsevents/press/monetary/20121212a.htm

Morgan, D. P. (1991). Will Just-In-Time Inventory Techniques Dampen Recessions? *Kansas City Fed - Economic Review* , 21-33.

Morgan, S., & Hurley, J. (2004). Internet pharmacy: prices on the up-and-up. *CMAJ* , vol. 170 no. 6.

Motley, B. (1998). Growth and Inflation: A Cross-Country Study. *FRBSF Economic Review* , Number 1, 15-28.

Myerson, R. B. (1991). *Game Theory : Analysis of Conflict*. Cambridge, Massachusetts: Harvard University Press.

Newbery, C. (2011, October 28). *Argentina Steps Up Capital Controls to Buffer Reserves*. Retrieved November 24, 2012, from Market News International: https://mninews.marketnews.com/content/argentina-steps-capital-controls-buffer-reserves?q=content/argentina-steps-capital-controls-buffer-reserves

Obama, B. (2012, July 13). (R. F. Department, Interviewer)

Pagliery, J. (2012, 2 21). *Firms turn to riskier financing*. Retrieved 11 1, 2012, from CNN Money: http://money.cnn.com/2012/02/17/smallbusiness/bank_loans_financing/index.htm

Paradox of thrift. (2012, November 14). Retrieved November 14, 2012, from Wikipedia: http://en.wikipedia.org/wiki/Paradox_of_thrift

Piketty, T., & Saez, E. (2003). Income Inequality in the United States, 1913-1998. *The Quarterly Journal of Economics, Vol. CXVIII, Issue 1* .

Rastello, S., & Raszewski, E. (2012, September 18). *IMF to Put Argentina on Path to Censure Over Inflation Data*. Retrieved November 24, 2012, from Bloomberg: http://www.bloomberg.com/news/2012-09-18/imf-to-put-argentina-on-path-toward-censure-over-economic-data.html

Reinhart, C. M., & Rogoff, K. (2011). *This Time is Different*. Princeton University Press.

Reinhart, C. M., & Smith, T. R. (n.d.). *Too much of a good thing: The macroeconomic effects of taxing capital inflows*. Retrieved from

Munich Personal RePEc Archive: http://mpra.ub.uni-muenchen.de/13234/1/reinhart_smith.pdf

Reitzel, J. D., Lyden, D. P., Roberts, N. J., & Severance, G. B. (1990). *Contemporary Business Law, Principles and Cases, 4th Ed.* New York: McGraw-Hill Publishing Company.

Remini, R. V. (1984). *Andrew Jackson; Volume Three The Course of American Democracy 1833-1845.* Baltimore, MD: The Johns Hopkins University Press.

Reuer, J. J., & Tong, T. W. (2007). *Real Options Theory.* Elsevier JAI.

Rodrik, D. (2006). *The Social Cost of Foreign Exchange Reserves.* Cambridge, MA: National Bureau of Economic Research.

Romero, S., & Minder, R. (2012, April 16). Argentina to Seize Control of Oil Company. *The New York Times* .

Russo, J. E., & Schoemaker, P. J. (1989). *Decision Traps : The Ten Barriers To Brilliant Decision-Making And How To Overcome Them.* New York: Simon & Schuster.

Saez, E. (2012, 3 2). *Striking it Richer.* Retrieved 5 18, 2013, from UC Berkeley: http://elsa.berkeley.edu/~saez/saez-UStopincomes-2010.pdf

Sales Tax Institute. (2012, November 1). Retrieved November 14, 2012, from Sales Tax Institute: http://www.salestaxinstitute.com/resources/rates

Samuelson, P. A., & Nordhaus, W. D. (2005). *Economics.* New York: McGraw-Hill/Irwin.

Sardoni, C. (2011). *Unemployment, Recession and Effective Demand.* Northampton, MA: Edward Elgar Publishing Inc.

Scallon, S. (2009, September 1). *Breaking the Bank.* Retrieved November 24, 2012, from The American Conservative: http://www.theamericanconservative.com/articles/breaking-the-bank/

Shedlock, M. M. (2010). *Defining Money Supply to Understand Its Actions.* Retrieved from Minyanville.com: http://www.minyanville.com/businessmarkets/articles/money-supply-austrian-true-on-demand/3/19/2010/id/27364?page=full

Sides, J. (2011, July). *Stories, Science, and Public Opinion about the Estate Tax.* Retrieved November 24, 2012, from George Washington University: http://home.gwu.edu/~jsides/estatetax.pdf

Small businesses turn to alternative lenders. (2012, 11 13). Retrieved 12 1, 2012, from USA Today: http://www.usatoday.com/story/money/business/2012/11/13/unconventional-business-loans/1650637/

Snowdon, C. (2011). *The Spirit Level Delusion.* Monday Books.

St. Louis Fed - FRED. (2012). Retrieved from Federal Reserve
    Economic Data: http://research.stlouisfed.org/fred2/

Sturzenegger, F., & Zettelmeyer, J. (2006). *Debt Defaults and Lessons
    from a Decade of Crises*. Cambridge, MA: The MIT Press.

Taylor, L. D. (2010). *Capital, Accumulation, and Money*. New York:
    Springer.

Thaler, R. H. (1993). *Advances in Behavioral Finance*. Russell Sage
    Foundation .

The Essentials of Negotiation. (2005). Boston, MA: Harvard Business
    School Press.

The Fair Tax Plan. (2012, November 24). Retrieved November 24, 2012,
    from Fair Tax:
    http://www.fairtax.org/site/PageServer?pagename=HowFairTaxWo
    rks

The Money Supply. (2012). Retrieved from Federal Reserve Bank of
    New York: http://www.ny.frb.org/aboutthefed/fedpoint/fed49.html

Tzu, S., & Griffith, S. B. (1971). *The Art of War*. Oxford University
    Press.

United States Census Bureau. (2011). *U.S. International Trade Data*.

*United States of America Long-Term Rating Lowered To 'AA+' Due To
    Political Risks, Rising Debt Burden; Outlook Negative*. (2011,
    August 5). Retrieved 4 12, 2013, from Standard and Poor's:
    http://www.standardandpoors.com/ratings/articles/en/us/?assetID=1
    245316529563

Vaggi, G., & Groenewegen, P. (2003). *A Concise History of Economic
    Thought*. New York: Palgrave Macmillan.

Viable Opposition. (2011, November 9). *Sovereign Debt Default:
    Learning Lessons from Argentina*. Retrieved November 24, 2012,
    from Viable Opposition:
    http://viableopposition.blogspot.com/2011/11/sovereign-debt-
    default-learning-lessons.html

Wachter, M. (2007, Summer). The Rise and Decline of Unions. *Cato
    Org - Regulation* .

Washington, R. (2010, August 23). Maybe it isn't China. *The Economist* .

Wijnholds, O. d. (2011). *Fighting Financial Fires; An IMF Insider
    Account*. New York: Palgrave Macmillan.

Wikipedia - Michal Kalecki. (2012). Retrieved from Wikipedia:
    http://en.wikipedia.org/wiki/Micha%C5%82_Kalecki

Wikiquote - Andrew Jackson. (2012, November 24). Retrieved
    November 24, 2012, from Wikiquote:
    http://en.wikiquote.org/wiki/Andrew_Jackson

Wilkinson, R., & Pickett, K. (2011). *The Spirit Level: Why Greater Equality Makes Societies Stronger.* Bloomsbury Press; Reprint edition.

(2011). *World Health Statistics.* WHO.

Worstall, T. (2012, February 3). That Giant Sucking Sound of Manufacturing Jobs Going to China. *Forbes* .

Yellen, J. L. (2005). *Productivity and Inflation.* San Francisco, CA: Federal Reserve Bank of San Francisco.

Yellen, J. L. (2006, November 6). *Speech to the Center for the Study of Democracy.* Retrieved November 14, 2012, from Federal Reserve Bank of San Francisco: http://www.frbsf.org/news/speeches/2006/1106.html

INDEX

ABOUT THE AUTHOR

Rick Puglisi has 23 years of financial research and trading experience, having held several senior international positions on Wall Street. His Wall St. experiences include financial modeling, multi-asset class risk management, and managing trading desks. He is currently the founder and managing member of a private investment management company.

Mr. Puglisi holds a Masters of Business Administration from Cornell University's Johnson Graduate School of Management ('91) as well as M.S. ('87) and B.S. ('86) degrees in Civil Engineering from the University of Minnesota.